★ ★

BUYING REAL ESTATE IN THE US
The Concise Guide for Canadians

★ ★

BUYING REAL ESTATE IN THE US
The Concise Guide for Canadians

Dale Walters, CPA, PFS, CFP®

Self-Counsel Press
(a division of)
International Self-Counsel Press Ltd.
USA   Canada

Self-Counsel Press acknowledges the financial support of the Government of Canada through the Canada Book Fund (CBF) for our publishing activities.

Printed in Canada.

First edition: 2011

Library and Archives Canada Cataloguing in Publication

Walters, Dale, 1958–

    Buying real estate in the US / Dale Walters.

    ISBN 978-1-77040-068-9

    1. House buying — United States. 2. Home ownership — United States. 3. Investments, Canadian — United States. 4. Real estate investment — Taxation — United States. — I. Title.

HD255.W27 2011   333.33'83   C2010-906874-2

Self-Counsel Press
(a division of)
International Self-Counsel Press Ltd.

1704 North State Street	1481 Charlotte Road
Bellingham, WA 98225	North Vancouver, BC V7J 1H1
USA	Canada

Contents

Samples

Tables

Notice to Readers

Laws are constantly changing. Every effort is made to keep this publication as current as possible. However, the author, the publisher, and the vendor of this book make no representations or warranties regarding the outcome or the use to which the information in this book is put and are not assuming any liability for any claims, losses, or damages arising out of the use of this book. The reader should not rely on the author or the publisher of this book for any professional advice. Please be sure that you have the most recent edition.

Prices, commissions, fees, and other costs mentioned in the text or shown in samples in this book probably do not reflect real costs where you live. Inflation and other factors, including geography, can cause the costs you might encounter to be much higher or even much lower than those we show. The dollar amounts shown are simply intended as representative examples.

Circular 230 Disclaimer: Nothing in this book is to be used or relied upon by anyone for the purposes of avoiding penalties that may be imposed on you under the Internal Revenue Code of 1986, as amended. Any statements contained within this book relating to any federal tax transaction or matter may not be used by any person to support the promotion or marketing to recommend any federal tax transaction. Everyone should seek advice based on their particular circumstances from an independent cross-border tax advisor. No one, without the express written permission, may use any part of this book in promoting, marketing, or recommending an arrangement relating to any federal tax matter to anyone else.

Acknowledgments

I have wanted to write a book for at least 20 years and now I finally have. I could hardly have done it at a more demanding time; running a fast-growing company, and still having kids at home, made this time one of the busiest of my career.

The initial inspiration for this book came from my business partner, Robert (Bob) Keats. He was already a successful author when I met him 17 years ago. Bob Keats is the author of a Canadian best-selling book titled *The Border Guide*, now in its tenth edition.

Ultimately, if it were not for the support, understanding, and inspiration of my wife, Charlene, and children, Elysha and Neal, I would not have been able to accomplish a large undertaking such as this. Their patience and encouragement to finish the book got me through nearly a year of writing, researching, and editing.

I also want to acknowledge the Keats, Connelly and Associates employees, past and present, on their contribution to this book. They have provided me with knowledge and encouragement at every step along the way. In particular, I want to thank Wayne Tibbetts, our Director of Tax Services; and David Levine, our International Tax Manager, for reviewing and providing input on several chapters.

Shant Epremian, a realtor and friend in Florida provided most of the information for the first chapter.

Lastly, I want to thank all of the clients I have worked with over the years. It is the clients who have put me in a position to be able to write a book on this topic in the first place; without them this book would not have been possible.

★ ★

Introduction

Buying a home in the United States is a goal for many Canadians so they can get some relief from the long and cold winters in Canada. Dreams of daily rounds of golf in the sunny and warm destinations of the US Sunbelt has inspired Canadians to buy second homes in places such as Palm Springs, California; Phoenix, Tucson, and Yuma, Arizona; San Padre Island, Texas; and numerous locations throughout Florida.

Now, with economic conditions being as they are, many more Canadians are looking to invest in US real estate. With US real estate prices severely depressed due in part to the worldwide economic crisis and bad US policies, the buying opportunity in the US has become a once in a lifetime event for everyone, not just Canadians. Combine the fact that the Canadian economy is healthy and the Canadian dollar is (at the time of writing) essentially at par with the US dollar, Canadians have unique buying opportunities that may never be seen again.

While plenty of opportunity exists, there are a number of potential pitfalls if you do not plan and use competent professionals to help you through the buying process. In many ways, the process seems obvious with few, if any, roadblocks. In fact, the process is so easy that many Canadians do not seek proper advice or get incorrect advice from people who do not specialize in this area.

An adage I have long lived by is "just because you can, doesn't mean you should," and that adage is particularly applicable in this situation. On almost a daily basis I get a question along the lines of, "Can I do that with the property?" The answer is nearly always, yes you can do that, *but you shouldn't* do that. For example, if you asked your realtor if you can own the property in your corporation, he or she would say yes (which is the correct answer), but the realtor would not know to add that you should not own the property in the corporation because it would cause a double taxation. If you get nothing else out of this book, I want you to get the fact that you need, first and foremost, to hire knowledgeable professionals to assist you through the process and to change your questions from, "Can I do this?" to "Should I do this?"

I believe you will find many issues addressed and answered in this book that you will not find in any other book on the subject. That is why I wrote this book: to provide useful and practical advice that was missing from other books. The book is written largely from a tax perspective, so the material is complex and ever changing.

While I will attempt to answer the most common questions, it is impossible to answer every possible question. Every situation is different; do not rely on the fact that your friend bought a house in a certain way and assume that way will work for you. To begin with, you don't know if your friend did it correctly in the first place. Additionally, your facts, circumstances, goals, and time frames will likely be different from your friend's. I strongly recommend that you seek advice that is customized to your particular situation.

When seeking advice, look for a professional with a substantial amount of cross-border experience. There is a clear pattern that can be seen among the Canadians I talk to; an advisor on one side of the border gives perfectly good advice for his or her country, but ultimately gives bad advice because he or she did not understand the implications on the other side of the border. It is imperative that your advisor fully understand the implications of his or her advice on both sides of the border.

I have tried to make a complicated and dry subject at least readable and hopefully interesting through the use of samples and tables summarizing my points. I have also added throughout the book "Notes" and "Cautions" to make sure you do not miss important points. At the end of the book there is a checklist for you to use when buying real estate in the US.

I wish you the best of luck in your real estate investing endeavors.

1
A RARE OPPORTUNITY

A Rare Opportunity

"It's too good to be true."

While this statement is usually true, it appears to not be the case when talking about the real estate investment opportunities that exist right now for Canadians in the United States. The combination of drastically reduced home prices, Canadian currency prices near an all-time high relative to the US dollar, and low financing options create what appears to be a once in a lifetime opportunity for Canadians to buy US real estate. Before we dive into the opportunities that exist, it is important to understand the genesis of these opportunities and why they exist.

1. How the Opportunity Was Created

Let's go back in time to about 2005; the stock market was hot, the housing market was on a steady climb, and the general consensus was that housing prices would continue to steadily climb month after month, year after year with no end in sight. People of all social classes jumped on this bandwagon and became real estate investment experts overnight as they proceeded to invest purely on emotion. Without much thought, experience, or education, they refinanced their homes, maxed out their credit cards, and used all their available savings in an effort to pour as much money as possible into their real estate purchases. Credit was extended with such ease that it was difficult to resist the temptation, making real estate investing seem like child's play.

Builders and developers could not keep up with demand and it was common for projects to sell out within days of being placed on the market. It was a bidding war; to the point where investors would commonly sell units that they had on deposit to other investors at a profit without ever taking possession. Keep in mind that these were multiple transactions on dwellings that were not even built! Housing projects were erected at such a fast pace that we had a shortage of drywall in the US and proceeded to import drywall from Asia. The good times had no end in sight, so why not jump right in?

Here was the problem: All good things do come to an end. The housing market started to level off and cool down in late 2006. At first, investors thought that the market was actually giving them a new opportunity to jump in before it continued its steady climb but in actual fact, the only thing that was ahead was several months of steady decline. Week after week, month after month, we saw a freefall in property values throughout much of the country. This crisis was led by states such as Florida, Arizona, and Nevada where prices were the most inflated.

Unfortunately the market turned so fast that it caught many investors by surprise. It was too late to change course for the hundreds of thousands of people who had either refinanced, or bought a second or third home or investment property to try and sell it because by this point there was already a surplus of inventory. The problem, however, was not so much the surplus inventory, but the surplus *in* inventory, plus the consumers' inability to pay for their properties due to large amounts of leverage. The combination of high leverage and declining property values created a situation in which owners could not sell because their mortgages were more than the value of the properties.

To make matters worse, the subprime or second-chance loans were widely sold during the height of the market. These loans were very popular and so easy to get that people often mocked, "If you had a pulse you could qualify for a mortgage!" These loans were so bad they are now called "toxic" loans. The types of loans written included the following:

- 40- or 50-year loans

- Adjustable Rate Mortgages (ARM)

- Option ARM loans

- Negative amortization loans

- No document loans

- Interest-only loans

- 100 percent+ financing loans

- Stated income stated assets loan

- No income no assets loans

- 80/20 loans

Someone could easily write a book just on the types of subprime or second-chance loans that were available, but my point is not to educate you on the types of loans; rather to give you a better idea of the options that were available to these consumers and the ease at which they were able to borrow money. Let's face it, when you are lending someone funds based on stated income and stated assets with no document verification, or you have to amortize the loan over 40 or 50 years so that the person can afford the payments, these are signs of trouble and it is evident that many consumers who should never have been given credit were extended credit.

Some will argue that lending institutions should have been more diligent when extending credit; others put the blame on the government for having weak oversight on these policies; and, finally, some blame the consumers themselves for being irrational and overextending themselves. Regardless of who is to blame, the important thing to keep in mind is that most people were not concerned about the type of loan they had, or the minimum payment they had to meet because everyone assumed that they would flip the property in 3, 6, or 12 months at a profit, and never actually had to deal with paying anything more than the interest on the note. What people failed to realize is that the slightest change in interest rates or the state of the economy would mean that they would be stuck with the mortgages and they could barely afford the interest let alone the principal payments. For this reason we began to see such an influx of delinquencies week after week, month after month. People could not sell their properties, and rates on their notes adjusted from interest only to principal and interest. To make matters worse, most loans had clauses that allowed lenders to add extra interest on loans if payment was received late.

By now I hope you understand how many Americans got into this mess, and will therefore appreciate the opportunity that currently exists in the distressed property market. The moral of the story is to remain rational and not to get caught up in the market hype.

2. The Three Types of Real Estate Transactions

The words "short sales" and "foreclosures" have become synonymous with "great deals." However, there are fundamental differences between them and it's important that you understand the differences before investing.

Caution: Remember that cheap does not always mean that it is a deal; it could be cheap for another reason. In addition, always have an exit strategy in mind when you are buying.

Generally speaking there are three types of real estate transactions:

1. Traditional sale

2. Short sale

3. Foreclosure or bank-owned property

The following sections include a brief review of each transaction.

2.1 Traditional sale

The traditional sale is the type of sale that you are used to if you have ever purchased a property. It involves two parties — the buyers and the sellers. The sellers may or may not have a mortgage on their property but the important thing to understand is that the amount of the note or mortgage does not exceed the sale price of the property. In this case the sellers at their *sole discretion* can sell the property at a price that is convenient for them and do not need third-party or lender approval to do so, because the proceeds from the sale more than cover all expenses including the repayment of the note.

2.2 Short sale

A short sale is unique in the sense that the sellers of the property are facing financial distress. Often they are late on their mortgage payments due to any number of reasons, and they are trying to sell the house for less money than is actually owed on the note or mortgage. For example:

Mr. and Mrs. Smith purchased their home at the height of the market in 2005 for $300,000. At the time they really could only afford a $200,000 home but they were lured into a five-year, interest-only loan that made them feel that they could afford a $300,000 home because of the low interest payments. They proceeded to purchase their home with 0 percent down-payment and, therefore, owed the full $300,000 plus closing costs, for a total of about $310,000. The Smiths had opted for an Adjustable Rate Mortgage (ARM), where after five years the rate adjusted to prime plus 5 percent.

Fast forward five years, Mr. Smith loses his job, and to make matters worse his mortgage payments tripled overnight because of the adjustment in rate. Now the family definitely can't afford the new mortgage payments and are forced to sell their home. Unfortunately, because of market conditions and declining property values, it would be impossible for them to sell their house for the amount of the mortgage. Therefore they are selling the property for a shortfall which constitutes a short sale.

When you hear about the term "being upside down," this is what's being referred to. Very simplistically, a short sale is when there is a sale and the person owes more on the property than the property is worth.

You are probably wondering why this is relevant. Well, it's important that as a buyer you understand that when you put an offer on the Smiths' residence, for example, you are in fact facing a situation where the sale is subject to third-party approval (i.e., the lender or lenders).

Here is how a short sale works: Like a traditional sale, you would put an offer on the property that interests you and request that the selling party accept the terms or price of the sale. So far it's the same process as a traditional sale; however, now that you placed your offer for the property, both the lender and the owners must decide whether they will allow the property to be sold at this price or not. Remember the lenders are potentially taking a large loss on this property (the difference between the outstanding mortgage and the sales price). This is the part that can be very time consuming and frustrating, if you work with a realtor who does not understand the negotiation process and all of the things that need to be provided to the bank to help it make its decision.

Now let's twist this situation slightly and assume that two years after the property was purchased, the Smiths refinanced their home and took a second mortgage. Now both mortgagees need to agree to a payoff amount for the deal to happen since we know that there are not enough funds to cover both loans at the current purchase price. It is also important to note that both the first and second mortgage holders need to agree on a settlement before the short sale can be approved and the transaction can occur.

One more common caveat: Beware when the mortgage holder requires the sellers to sign off on a personal promissory note. The promissory note is the bank's way of trying to recoup loses in the future (over five or ten years) for clients who did short sales. This often delays the process because the seller doing the short sale may strongly oppose the personal promissory; the point of the short sale is to wipe out all ties to the property in question. Because this is often unexpected to clients there is usually a delay in getting this promissory note signed. The clients feel that the bank may come after the sellers for the entire amount of the short sale. At that point some people will opt out of the short sale entirely simply because they are misinformed. The reasons behind why it may or may not be required are complex and not important for you to understand; however, as the buyer, it is important for you to understand that this situation may delay the process.

These are only two common reasons that short sales do take time and do require patience to get a final approval, but the time and frustration can be justified by the potential deal that one may get.

There are many realtors who think they understand this process, but few that have actually mastered it. Look for real estate professionals who have seen firsthand horror stories of clients purchasing distressed properties and can guide you through the numerous issues. Needless to say this negotiation process requires a certain skill and method to ensure a smooth transaction and thus it is important that you select a real estate professional to represent you in this purchase. Do not attempt this on your own. Certain key steps early in the process can help mitigate the time it takes to get the short sale approved.

2.3 Foreclosure or bank-owned property

In simplistic terms, a foreclosure is a property where the note bearer has forcefully evicted the inhabitants for nonpayment of their mortgages. Basically if we take the previous example with the Smith family and assume they stopped paying their mortgage, eventually they would be driven out of their home and the bank would take over the property. Since lenders are not in the business of owning property, they proceed to sell the property in an *as is* condition on the open market.

Bank properties are often the fastest deals to close, but have their own challenges because they are often properties that have not been lived in for a while and therefore need attention to bring them up to living standards. In some markets, approximately one-half of all resales are foreclosures. For example, in September 2010, 46 percent of the greater Phoenix market's single family home resales were foreclosures.

3. The Window of Opportunity

Opportunities will always exist in real estate; however, most professionals believe that the window of opportunity that currently exists may be short-lived. This is primarily because lenders are not extending credit today like they were in the past; they are being very prudent and as a result the chances of consumers defaulting on loans will be greatly minimized. One of the main reasons the US got into this mess was the so-called subprime or second-chance mortgages. I believe that we will not again see this abundance of distressed properties for a long time.

The three rules in real estate have always been and will always be: location, location, location. No matter what part of the country you are thinking of investing in, my professional opinion is that it is always worth spending a little extra when you are buying to get a desirable location. Not all bargains are good deals. As the buyer you are in the driver's seat. There is an abundance of inventory, the Canadian dollar is near parity, and interest rates are very low. There are tremendous deals to take advantage of that are 30 to 70 percent less, relative to the height of the market, depending on location and property type. The time to invest is now; do not let this opportunity pass you by, but remember that you can still lose money if you are not careful.

In closing, I would like to stress the importance of working with reputable real estate professionals. The professionals that you surround yourself with in making this important choice can make a world of difference. Decisions are always better made when you are well informed of the process; it never hurts to be too well informed.

Being well informed is more than finding the right property, in the right location, at the right price. You have to understand how best to take title to the property, and consider what the tax implications are when you own, when you sell, and when you die. These items and more will be covered in the following chapters.

2

WAYS OF OWNING REAL ESTATE

Ways of Owning Real Estate

When buying real estate in the US there are two general ways in which title can be taken; directly by the individual(s), or indirectly through an entity such as a corporation, partnership, or trust. I further divide indirect ownership into Canadian entities and US entities.

It is important that you know and understand your options and remember that there are no one-size-fits-all solutions. It is uncommon to find a solution that has all positive and no negative attributes. You need to talk to a knowledgeable advisor to review your goals and options to determine which solution works best for your situation. This chapter discusses the most common ways to own property as well as the pros and cons of each.

Important: When deciding on the type of entity structure, always keep in mind that you want the simplest structure that will accomplish the goal. Beware that some advisors seem to make things more complicated than they need to be. Whether the reason is to look smart or to justify their fee, the bottom line is that (within reason) by keeping it as simple as you can, you save money and headaches. Of course, some complexity may be either necessary or desired; just be sure you know why the complexity is recommended. More complex situations may require entities and strategies not discussed here. In complex situations, consult with a knowledgeable advisor.

1. Direct Ownership through an Individual or Individuals

The simplest way to buy a piece of real estate is to title the property directly in your name or you and your spouse's names. Of course, direct ownership is not limited to two people or to a husband and wife; there can be many individuals named on the title. While it is possible to name any number of individuals on a title, I would typically recommend establishing some sort of entity if you name anyone other than a spouse.

There are two main reasons for using an entity when someone other than your spouse will be an owner. The first reason is to protect your assets from lawsuits or the claims of the creditors of your co-owners. For example, if your co-owner gets a divorce, the spouse could get one-half of his or her share of the property. Other problems include bankruptcy and various judgments and lawsuits against the co-owner that could cause you to become an owner of the property with a complete stranger, or it might cause a forced sale at an inopportune time.

If you are considering naming a child as co-owner to avoid probate, nine states allow for the property to be transferred on death directly to a beneficiary without probate. This is also known as a beneficiary deed. Those nine states are Arizona, Colorado, Kansas, Missouri, Nevada, New Mexico, Arkansas, Ohio, and Wisconsin. A beneficiary deed is similar to any other beneficiary designation you use such as with your registered accounts or life insurance. The beneficiary can be changed at any time before death. If the property is held jointly, the beneficiary receives the property after the second person's death.

A beneficiary deed can be drawn up by you or an attorney. The title company will record the deed.

One thing to keep in mind is that the beneficiary can be changed anytime up to the second person's death. While flexibility can be a good thing in most situations, you may not want to use a beneficiary deed in all situations. For example, if in a second marriage with kids from previous marriages, you may not want your surviving spouse to have the ability to change the beneficiary and exclude your children.

2. Types of Ownership

Not every state allows property ownership in all possible ways. In general, there are two types of laws under which to own property depending on the state; they are called *community property law* states and *common-law* states. Community property law states are Arizona, California, Idaho, Louisiana, Nevada, New Mexico, Texas, Washington, and Wisconsin. There are two different ways you can purchase an asset using community property laws; *community property* and *community property with rights of survivorship*. Definitions are discussed in the following sections.

2.1 Community property

In community property states only, married couples can take ownership of property as community property. In this case, they will each own a half interest in the property. Unlike joint tenants, the owners can pass their interest (half) by will or trust upon death and will *not* avoid probate (see section **2.3**).

2.2 Community property with rights of survivorship

Certain community property states allow married couples to own property as community property with rights of survivorship. Like community property, the couple will each own a half interest in the property; however, when one person dies the survivor will automatically own the entire property and avoid probate.

2.3 Ways to purchase an asset in common-law property states

There are three ways to purchase an asset in common-law property states; a description of each is below:

➤ **Joint tenancy:** The most common way for couples to own property is as joint tenants, which means that each person owns an equal share in the property. If one owner dies, the survivor will then own the entire property by *right of survivorship.* The surviving joint tenant receives the property automatically. This means that the property will avoid the probate process and the associated fees.

➤ **Tenancy by the entirety:** In about half of the states, married couples can own property as tenants by the entirety. Like joint tenants, this form of ownership means that the surviving spouse owns the entire property and avoids probate. The primary difference between tenancy by the entirety and joint tenancy is that joint tenants may deal with the property as they wish. If one joint tenant decides to convey his or her interest in the property, that interest can be conveyed, and the joint tenancy can be destroyed. In tenancy by the entirety, each tenant effectively owns the entire estate. Therefore, neither can deal with the property independently of the other.

➤ **Tenancy in common:** Multiple owners can be listed as tenants in common. These owners can divide their interests in unequal percentages such as 80/20. The property does not transfer automatically at death and therefore does not avoid probate.

Joint tenants with rights of survivorship or community property with rights of survivorship are the two most common ways for spouses to own property directly. In both cases the property passes automatically to the surviving spouse and avoids probate. There are some differences in the rights of spouses, so if this is a concern, please consult an attorney for the specific differences.

When possible, owning property as community property with rights of survivorship is typically preferable. The reason has to do with income taxes due at death. When a couple owns property as joints tenants and one spouse dies, that person's cost basis in his or her half of the property gets adjusted to fair market value (FMV) at the date of death. However, couples owning property as community property with rights of survivorship will have cost basis of the entire property (100 percent versus 50 percent) adjusted to FMV.

Community property with rights of survivorship is typically preferable to community property without the rights of survivorship because the expenses of probate are avoided. If you recall, the difference between the two forms of community property is that with rights of survivorship, the survivor automatically owns the entire property and avoids probate. You want to avoid a multi-country probate whenever possible. Probate costs are the cost of settling your estate (mostly legal). Any assets that have to be passed to your heirs via your will are subject to probate. Take a look at the following example:

John and Carol Smith bought a house for $200,000. This means that essentially they bought the house for $100,000 each. Five years later John dies when the house is worth $300,000. On the date of death they owned a property worth $150,000 to each of them and each of them had a cost basis of $100,000, giving them each a gain of $50,000.

If the house was bought with the parties as joint tenants, only John's half would have its basis adjusted to FMV. This means that the half Carol receives from John has its cost basis adjusted from $100,000 to $150,000. Carol continues to retain her cost basis of $100,000. She now owns the entire property worth $300,000, with a cost basis of $250,000 (Carol's $100,000 plus John's $150,000). Carol could sell the property at this time and incur a gain of $50,000. **Note:** This adjustment to FMV applies only in the US.

If the house was bought as community property or as community property with rights of survivorship, both halves would be adjusted at the first death. This means that Carol would inherit the property with a $300,000 cost basis (FMV = $300,000 and basis is adjusted to FMV). This wipes out all capital gains as of John's death. Carol could sell the property at that time and incur no capital gains.

Caution: If the property declines in value, the cost basis also declines. In the above community property example, if the property declined to $150,000 at John's death, Carol would inherit the property with a basis of $150,000 — a loss of basis of $50,000. Whereas if they owned the property as joint tenants, the basis would be $175,000 (John's basis is adjusted to half of the FMV and Carol retains her $100,000 basis), leaving a $25,000 capital loss that could be taken if Carol sold the property at that time.

3. Indirect Ownership Using Canadian Entities

This section explains the pros and cons of owning US real estate in three different types of Canadian entities — a corporation, a limited partnership, and a trust. The most important thing to remember is that what works in Canada may not work in the US and what works in the US may not work in Canada. Do not assume the rules are the same in both countries; typically they are not.

Note: Canadian corporations, limited partnerships, and Canadian trusts are generally not recommended entities with which to buy US real estate.

3.1 Canadian corporation

A Canadian corporation is probably the most commonly suggested way of owning US real estate. I believe this is because the use of a Canadian corporation is familiar and convenient. In addition, if the corporation is appropriate and you already have a corporation, it saves the cost of forming an additional entity to own the property. However, there are some significant reasons not to use a Canadian corporation when buying US real estate. The disadvantages are that it will cause double taxation, and generally eliminate the possibility of special capital gains tax treatment.

A Canadian corporation doing business in the US will have to file IRS Form 1120-F: US Income Tax Return of a Foreign Corporation. US tax law imposes a double tax on corporations in this way. Dividends paid to shareholders are not deductible by the corporation (first tax) and the recipients have to pay tax on the full dividend (second tax).

Note: A Canadian corporation is doing business in the US, even if the home is purchased for personal use, when it purchases real estate.

Another issue that has come up recently is that newly formed single-purpose corporations are not allowed to own real estate. If you do own an older corporation that would allow the ownership of real estate, you still need to be careful to follow the rules so that your corporation does not become a disallowed entity. This can happen if your corporation owns a home in which you live in (or otherwise receive personal benefits) and you do not pay fair market rent or take into income the value of the fair market rent. All in all, while there are some exceptions, I do not recommend buying US real estate in a Canadian corporation in most cases.

3.2 Canadian limited partnership

A Canadian limited partnership is a common way for sophisticated Canadian investors to buy real estate in Canada, but few Canadians own limited partnerships. While a Canadian limited partnership could work when buying US real estate, there are some reasons I would not suggest their use, especially if you don't already have one.

If you are doing business in the US it is better to have an entity in the state in which you own the property in case legal issues arise. It would be better to have an attorney and an entity in the state in which the dispute arises rather than try to have a Canadian attorney hire local attorneys and learn local laws.

Another matter that arises occasionally is the confusion or even outright refusal to work with a foreign entity by some institutions; not because of some sort of prejudice, but because of fear of the unknown. Rather than learn the differences in the rules when dealing with a foreign entity, they take the path of least resistance and refuse to work with the foreign entity.

3.3 Canadian inter vivos trusts

A Canadian trust is the least popular way for a Canadian to buy real estate in the US. The only reason someone would consider using a Canadian trust is to avoid US nonresident estate tax. However, there are good reasons for not using a trust, and they are higher tax rates and a deemed sale every 21 years. A deemed sale means that the property in the trust is treated as if it were (deemed) sold at fair market value (FMV). The resulting gain or loss is reported on the trust tax return. To make matters worse, if the assets are not actually sold, the gain is taxed at ordinary income tax rates and does not receive the benefit of the favorable capital gains tax rate (currently one-half the ordinary tax rate).

4. Indirect Ownership Using US Entities

This section explains the pros and cons of owning US real estate through some of the most common types of US entities — a Limited Liability Company, a corporation, a revocable living trust, a limited liability partnership, and a limited liability limited partnership. Do not assume the rules are the same in both Canada and the US; typically they are not.

4.1 Limited Liability Company (LLC)

A Limited Liability Company (LLC) is commonly used by Americans to purchase real estate and is often, but incorrectly, recommended to Canadians when they are buying real estate in the US. The fundamental problem with Canadians using LLCs is that the US and Canada treat the LLC differently.

An LLC is a hybrid entity, meaning that in the US it can be treated as a partnership, a corporation, or if there is only a single member (i.e., partner), as no entity at all, which is referred to as a disregarded entity.

Canada treats the income from an LLC similar to that of a Canadian corporation. Canada will tax only the distributions from the LLC, whereas the US will tax the net income regardless of whether or not distributions were made. This can result in a mismatch in the timing of foreign taxes and could therefore create a situation in which the same income is taxed twice.

As a member of an LLC, you will be required to file a US Return of Partnership Income (Form 1065) and an individual Nonresident Alien Income Tax Return (Form 1040NR). You may also be required to file separate state income tax returns.

Caution: An LLC is the worst way for a Canadian to purchase US real estate. If you have already used an LLC to purchase US real estate, consult a cross-border tax professional about the best way to correct the situation.

4.2 US Corporation

There are two types of corporations in the US: the general corporation known as a C corporation and the small-business corporation, known as an S corporation. S corporations do not allow foreign shareholders, therefore I will only be referring to C corporations.

A US corporation can be used in certain limited situations, but in general should be avoided when buying US real estate.

Unlike in Canada, there are very few good reasons for having a US corporation for any business except for the very largest; the reason is double taxation. Money earned in a corporation is taxed at the corporate level because there is no deduction for dividends paid, and there is also tax at the individual level. There is no dividend credit similar to that provided in Canada; the income is simply taxed twice. Another reason to avoid a corporation is the loss of the favorable capital gains tax rate when the gain occurs within a corporation. A US corporation is, in my opinion, the second worst way in which Canadians can buy real estate in the US.

As a shareholder of a US corporation, you will be required to file a US Corporation Income Tax Return (Form 1120). You may also be required to file separate state income tax returns.

4.3 Revocable living trust

A revocable living trust (or simply living trust) can be used and can provide a number of benefits in the right circumstances. The circumstances in which the living trust is best is where you are buying a second home with a value of $750,000 USD or more. If there will be any business activity such as rental, then a different entity should be considered to help protect you from personal liability. The reason for the $750,000 minimum is simply a cost-benefit analysis.

One thing you are trying to avoid with the living trust is the cost of probate. Probate fees are the cost of settling your estate. Any assets that have to be passed to your heirs via your will may be subject to probate. A living trust allows the assets to pass directly to your heirs and avoid your will and therefore probate. You have to weigh the cost of establishing the trust versus the cost of probate. In most states, probate cannot be easily avoided by other means, so a living trust is a viable solution. However, as I mentioned in section 1., when talking about direct ownership, nine states allow real estate to be transferred on death directly to the beneficiary (beneficiary deed). In those states, a trust is not needed to avoid probate, if the beneficiary deed is used.

If a living trust seems appropriate and you are considering its use, then I recommend that you look into the Cross Border Trust℠ offered by cross-border attorney David Altro. He wrote the book *Owning US Property — The Canadian Way*. In his book, Altro describes the many benefits of the Cross Border Trust.

The Cross Border Trust does not require additional tax forms to be filed. You will file a Canadian Simplified Individual Tax Return (Form T1), and an individual Nonresident Alien Income Tax Return (Form 1040NR) in the US when the property is sold.

4.4 Limited Liability Partnership (LLP) and Limited Liability Limited Partnership (LLLP)

A Limited Liability Partnership (LLP) is the entity I recommend for couples buying US real estate that will be turned into rentals. I believe the LLP provides the best combination of ease of use, tax benefits, and liability protection available in any one entity. An LLP is essentially a general partnership that provides limited liability to the partners.

A Limited Liability Limited Partnership (LLLP) is a limited partnership that provides limited liability to the general partner. I recommend this when either additional liability protection is needed or if you are investing with partners who are not your spouse, or the other half of any legally recognized couple in Canada. An LLLP would be used with people you are going into business with, that do not already have a legal right to your assets.

As a member of an LLP or LLLP, you will be required to file a Return of Partnership Income (Form 1065) and an individual Nonresident Alien Income Tax Return (Form 1040NR) in the US. You may also be required to file a separate state income tax return. Any tax you pay with your 1040NR can be used as a credit against your Canadian income tax.

Note: The preferred way of owning rental property in the US for couples is an LLP, and for non legally recognized couples the LLLP is preferred.

Table 1
SUMMARY OF THE PROS AND CONS OF EACH OWNERSHIP TYPE

Type of Ownership	Pros	Cons	Conclusion
Direct Ownership			
Community Property	Simple, no cost, potential capital gain tax advantage at first death, bank financing available	Probate expenses, only available in certain states, no liability protection	Community property with rights of survivorship is typically preferred when owning directly and where available
Community Property with Rights of Survivorship	Simple, no cost, potential capital gain tax advantage at first death, no probate at first death, bank financing available	Must pass directly to surviving spouse, only available in certain states, no liability protection	Where direct ownership is desired, preferred where available
Joint Tenants with Rights of Survivorship	Simple, no cost, bank financing available, no probate at first death	No potential capital gain advantage at death, no liability protection	Where direct ownership is desired and community property is not available, typically the preferred choice
Tenancy in common	Simple, no cost, can be used with non-spouses and multiple owners, bank financing available	No potential capital gain advantage at death, no liability protection	Preferred when direct ownership is desired and a couple is not married according to US law. I would avoid this with multiple owners and use a partnership instead.
Indirect Ownership			
Canadian Corporation	Avoids US nonresident estate tax, avoids US probate	Higher taxes, costs, complexity, unable to obtain mortgage	Recommend in very limited situations
Canadian Limited Partnership	Avoids US nonresident estate tax	Costs, complexity, unable to obtain mortgage	Recommend in very limited situations
Canadian Trust	Avoids US nonresident estate tax	Costs, complexity, 21-year step-up, lose control, unable to obtain mortgage	There are better solutions

Table 1 — Continued

US Limited Liability Company	Asset protection	Costs, complexity, higher taxes	Never use
US Corporation	Asset protection	Costs, complexity, higher taxation	Recommend in only very limited situations and in conjunction with a Canadian Corporation.
US Revocable Trust	Avoids probate, other potential benefits for next generation, can obtain mortgage	Cost to establish, no asset protection	A Cross Border Trust is best used when second home and the value is at least $750,000. A traditional US revocable living trust is not recommended because there are less expensive ways of avoiding probate.
US Limited Liability Partnership	Asset protection, no double taxation	Costs, limited complexity	When asset protection is desired, preferred method for couples
US Limited Liability Limited Partnership	Asset protection, no double taxation	Costs, limited complexity, not available in all states	When asset protection is desired, preferred method for those that are not couples.

3
INCOME TAXES

Income Taxes

As I discussed in Chapter 2, how you own a property may have an effect on how you are ultimately taxed. Different ways of owning property can lead to different tax outcomes.

There are a number of different issues to be considered when it comes to income taxes. Not only is there income tax on the rent, but there is a capital gains tax on the sale, the availability of foreign tax credits, and the tax filing requirements, to name the most important considerations. There is also potential US nonresident estate tax that has to be considered; however, we'll save that discussion for Chapter 4.

Note: It is important to look at all of the costs of investing in one state verses another. Florida has very high personal property tax rates to make up for its lack of income tax. Florida also has high insurance costs. California has both high income tax and insurance rates.

1. The Basics

Many of the people I talk to have the same question: "Will having rental income in the US cause my worldwide income to be taxable in the US?" The answer is absolutely not! The nonresident tax system is designed to tax nonresident companies and individuals on their US income only.

It is important to remember, as you think about US tax as a Canadian, that there are two different sources of laws that everyone must consider. The first set of laws is the *Internal Revenue Code* (IRC). Similar to the *Income Tax Act* (ITA) in Canada, the IRC is the set of laws that dictates the who, what, when, and how of taxes in the US.

The second set of laws is the US-Canada Income Tax Convention (Treaty). Some of the more important benefits the treaty provides include reducing or eliminating double taxation, identifying which country has taxing priority, improved compliance with tax laws, and creating consistency while improving certainty for taxpayers with international dealings.

Because the purpose of the Treaty is to modify when, how, and if certain income will be taxed, it is natural that there will be differences between the IRC and the Treaty; that is where much of the confusion comes from. The IRC is the default law and as a taxpayer you must elect to take advantage of the various Treaty provisions from which you wish to benefit. In most situations, you will want to make those elections because it is beneficial to be taxed according to the Treaty. For example, the IRC stipulates that a 30 percent withholding tax rate applies to the gross rental income earned in the US by nonresident aliens. The US-Canada Treaty allows you to take advantage of lower withholding on rent by having the tax apply to the net profits, rather than the gross rents (30 percent of the net versus 30 percent of the gross). To make a Treaty election, use the form Treaty-Based Return Position Disclosure (Form 8833). See Sample 1.

Sample 1
TREATY-BASED RETURN POSITION DISCLOSURE (FORM 8833)

Form 8833
(Rev. August 2006)
Department of the Treasury
Internal Revenue Service

Treaty-Based Return Position Disclosure
Under Section 6114 or 7701(b)

▶ **Attach to your tax return.**

OMB No. 1545-1354

Attach a separate Form 8833 for each treaty-based return position taken. Failure to disclose a treaty-based return position may result in a penalty of $1,000 ($10,000 in the case of a C corporation) (see section 6712).

Name

U.S. taxpayer identifying number

Address in country of residence

Address in the United States

Check one or both of the following boxes as applicable:

- The taxpayer is disclosing a treaty-based return position as required by section 6114 . . . . ▶ ☐

- The taxpayer is a dual-resident taxpayer and is disclosing a treaty-based return position as required by
  Regulations section 301.7701(b)-7 . . . . ▶ ☐

Check this box if the taxpayer is a U.S. citizen or resident or is incorporated in the United States . . . . ▶ ☐

1	Enter the specific treaty position relied on:	**3** Name, identifying number (if available to the taxpayer), and address in the United States of the payor of the income (if fixed or determinable annual or periodical). See instructions.
a	Treaty country	
b	Article(s)	
2	List the Internal Revenue Code provision(s) overruled or modified by the treaty-based return position	

4 List the provision(s) of the limitation on benefits article (if any) in the treaty that the taxpayer relies on to prevent application of that article ▶

5 Explain the treaty-based return position taken. Include a brief summary of the facts on which it is based. Also, list the nature and amount (or a reasonable estimate) of gross receipts, each separate gross payment, each separate gross income item, or other item (as applicable) for which the treaty benefit is claimed ....

....

....

....

....

....

....

....

....

....

....

....

....

....

....

....

....

....

....

....

....

....

....

....

....

....

For Paperwork Reduction Act Notice, see page 3.

Cat. No. 14895L

Form **8833** (Rev. 8-2006)

There may be times when the Treaty and the IRC conflict, in which case, the long-standing policy of the US is to settle the issue using the "last in line" philosophy. Last in line means the last law to have been passed will be the law that is used. The theory is that lawmakers, when passing the new law, took into consideration all of the issues and potential conflicts, and decided this current law being passed is the latest and greatest thinking on the issue, and therefore takes precedent over any other law on the same subject.

For example, a few years ago, taxpayers who had foreign tax credits and were subject to the Alternative Minimum Tax (AMT), were only able to reduce their regular tax liability by a maximum of 90 percent, if they were subject to AMT. As mentioned before, one of the main objectives of the Treaty is to avoid double taxation. To the extent taxpayers were subject to this AMT limitation on foreign tax credits, there was double taxation. There was some question as to which law took precedent. As it turned out, the AMT law had been passed after the last amendment to the Treaty, therefore the double tax stood as the correct legal answer.

The IRS talks about income that is effectively connected with a trade or business. Throughout the IRC and the Treaty you will see the term "effectively connected income," without the words "trade or business" connected to it. Whenever you see or hear people talk about effectively connected income, know that they mean from a trade or business. Rental income is an example of effectively connected income.

It is not my intention to cover every possible scenario in this chapter or even in this book; my intention is to illustrate only the situations most Canadians will encounter. Consult Internal Revenue Service Publication 515, *Withholding of Tax on Nonresident Aliens and Foreign Entities,* or consult a US-Canada tax specialist if you have a situation that is not covered here.

Note: You can find IRS forms at www.irs.gov/app/picklist/list/formsInstructions.html.

2. Rental Income

Whenever you collect a fee for use of your property, even if it's for only one day, you have rental income. It is important that you understand that any rental income received is taxable in both the US and Canada. Any tax paid in the US is used as a credit against your Canadian tax.

I have people tell me that they do not report the rental income in the US because they are reporting the income in Canada, or they do not report in Canada because they report the income in the US, but this is not the correct way to report the income; it must be reported in the US (where it was earned) and in Canada (where you live and pay taxes on a worldwide basis).

2.1 Direct ownership

If you were to own a rental property directly in your name or jointly with another person, the IRS specified withholding rate is 30 percent on the gross revenue of the rental activity. Revenue is defined as the gross amount of money coming into the business, before any expenses are taken. However, the Treaty allows you to elect to withhold on the profit of the rental business. Profit is defined as revenue less expenses. Non-accountants many times refer to profit as *income* or *net income*.

As a nonresident owner of a rental property, you will normally hire a property manager to take care of the day-to-day activities of the rental. The property manager will be your US withholding agent and as such will be required to withhold the necessary tax. When searching for property managers, be sure the manager understands his or her obligation to withhold and how to complete the necessary forms.

There are many peculiarities in the US tax system and two of them apply in the case of withholding on rentals. If you do not hire a property manager, technically your tenant is the withholding agent. Publication 515, *Withholding of Tax on*

Nonresident Aliens and Foreign Entities states: "Generally, the US person who pays an amount subject to nonresident alien (NRA) withholding is the person responsible for withholding." This is peculiar primarily because this places the tenant in a potentially adversarial role with you, the owner. If I were a tenant, I would neither want to be personally liable for the withholding tax, nor would I want to spend my time learning the applicable laws and filing the necessary tax forms or money to hire an accountant. Nonetheless, from a legal point of view, that is the position the tenant would be in.

The other peculiarity is that while you are allowed to file an election to be taxed on your profits (net income), that election is made when you file your US tax return (US Nonresident Alien Income Tax Return — Form 1040NR) sometime the following year. Yet, the withholding agent is generally required to withhold 30 percent of the rent amount from each payment, barring an election to the contrary.

Form 1040NR is the return nonresident individuals file in the US to report their US income. While the form may look relatively easy to complete because of its brevity, it can be challenging even for an experienced tax preparer due to the many possible elections that can be made. (See Sample 2.)

So how do you deal with this issue? Regardless of whether you are using a property manager or renting the property directly, you, as the owner, should provide the manager or tenant with IRS Certificate of Foreign Person's Claim That Income Is Effectively Connected With the Conduct of a Trade or Business in the United States (Form W-8ECI), indicating that the income is effectively connected with a US trade or business and therefore not subject to withholding tax. (See Sample 3.)

Since Form W-8ECI asks for your Individual Taxpayer Identification Number (ITIN), you will need to obtain an ITIN by filing an Application for IRS Individual Taxpayer Identification Number (Form W-7). The first question you are asked is "Reason you are submitting Form W-7." You will most likely

US NONRESIDENT ALIEN INCOME TAX RETURN (FORM 1040NR)

Form **1040NR**	**U.S. Nonresident Alien Income Tax Return**	OMB No. 1545-0074
Department of the Treasury Internal Revenue Service	For the year January 1–December 31, 2010, or other tax year beginning , 2010, and ending , 20	**2010**

Please print or type.

Your first name and initial	Last name	Identifying number (see instructions)
Present home address (number, street, and apt. no., or rural route). If you have a P.O. box, see instructions.		Check if: ☐ Individual ☐ Estate or Trust
City, town or post office, state, and ZIP code. If you have a foreign address, see instructions.		

Country ▶

Filing Status

Check only one box.

1 ☐ Single resident of Canada or Mexico or single U.S. national
2 ☐ Other single nonresident alien
3 ☐ Married resident of Canada or Mexico or married U.S. national
4 ☐ Married resident of South Korea
5 ☐ Other married nonresident alien
6 ☐ Qualifying widow(er) with dependent child (see instructions)

If you checked box 3 or 4 above, enter the information below.

(i) Spouse's first name and initial	(ii) Spouse's last name	(iii) Spouse's identifying number

Exemptions

If more than four dependents, see instructions.

7a ☐ **Yourself.** If someone can claim you as a dependent, **do not** check box 7a . . . . ⎫ Boxes checked on 7a and 7b ____
 b ☐ **Spouse.** Check box 7b only if you checked box 3 or 4 above **and** your spouse **did not** have any U.S. gross income . . . . ⎭

c **Dependents:** (see instructions) (1) First name Last name	(2) Dependent's identifying number	(3) Dependent's relationship to you	(4) ✔ If qualifying child for child tax credit (see page 9)	No. of children on 7c who:
	: :		☐	• lived with you ____
	: :		☐	• did not live with you due to divorce or separation ____
	: :		☐	Dependents on 7c not entered above ____
	: :		☐	

d Total number of exemptions claimed . . . . | Add numbers on lines above ▶ ☐

Income Effectively Connected With U.S. Trade/ Business

Attach Form(s) W-2, 1042-S, SSA-1042S, RRB-1042S, and 8288-A here. Also attach Form(s) 1099-R if tax was withheld.

Enclose, but do not attach, any payment.

8	Wages, salaries, tips, etc. Attach Form(s) W-2	**8**	
9a	Taxable interest.	**9a**	
b	Tax-exempt interest. **Do not** include on line 9a . . .	**9b**	
10a	Ordinary dividends	**10a**	
b	Qualified dividends (see instructions)	**10b**	
11	Taxable refunds, credits, or offsets of state and local income taxes (see instructions) .	**11**	
12	Scholarship and fellowship grants. Attach Form(s) 1042-S or required statement (see instructions)	**12**	
13	Business income or (loss). Attach Schedule C or C-EZ (Form 1040)	**13**	
14	Capital gain or (loss). Attach Schedule D (Form 1040) if required. If not required, check here ☐	**14**	
15	Other gains or (losses). Attach Form 4797	**15**	
16a	IRA distributions . . . **16a**	16b Taxable amount (see instructions)	**16b**	
17a	Pensions and annuities **17a**	17b Taxable amount (see instructions)	**17b**	
18	Rental real estate, royalties, partnerships, trusts, etc. Attach Schedule E (Form 1040)	**18**	
19	Farm income or (loss). Attach Schedule F (Form 1040)	**19**	
20	Unemployment compensation	**20**	
21	Other income. List type and amount (see instructions) _____	**21**	
22	Total income exempt by a treaty from page 5, Schedule OI, Item L (1)(e) . **22**		
23	Combine the amounts in the far right column for lines 8 through 21. This is your **total effectively connected income** . . . . ▶	**23**	

Adjusted Gross Income

24	Educator expenses (see instructions)	**24**	
25	Health savings account deduction. Attach Form 8889 .	**25**	
26	Moving expenses. Attach Form 3903	**26**	
27	One-half of self-employment tax. Attach Schedule SE (Form 1040)	**27**	
28	Self-employed SEP, SIMPLE, and qualified plans .	**28**	
29	Self-employed health insurance deduction (see instructions)	**29**	
30	Penalty on early withdrawal of savings	**30**	
31	Scholarship and fellowship grants excluded . . .	**31**	
32	IRA deduction (see instructions)	**32**	
33	Student loan interest deduction (see instructions) . . .	**33**	
34	Domestic production activities deduction. Attach Form 8903 . .	**34**	
35	Add lines 24 through 34	**35**	
36	Subtract line 35 from line 23. This is your **adjusted gross income**. . . . . ▶	**36**	

For Disclosure, Privacy Act, and Paperwork Reduction Act Notice, see instructions.   Cat. No. 11364D   Form **1040NR** (2010)

Form 1040NR (2010) Page **2**

Tax and Credits	37	Amount from line 36 (adjusted gross income)	37	
	38	**Itemized deductions** from page 3, Schedule A, line 17	38	
	39	Subtract line 38 from line 37	39	
	40	Exemptions (see instructions)	40	
	41	**Taxable income.** Subtract line 40 from line 39. If line 40 is more than line 39, enter -0-	41	
	42	**Tax** (see instructions). Check if any tax is from: a ☐ Form(s) 8814 b ☐ Form 4972	42	
	43	**Alternative minimum tax** (see instructions). Attach Form 6251 . . .	43	
	44	Add lines 42 and 43 . . . . ▶	44	

45	Foreign tax credit. Attach Form 1116 if required . . .	45	
46	Credit for child and dependent care expenses. Attach Form 2441	46	
47	Retirement savings contributions credit. Attach Form 8880	47	
48	Child tax credit (see instructions)	48	
49	Residential energy credits. Attach Form 5695	49	
50	Other credits from Form: a ☐ 3800 b ☐ 8801 c ☐ ___	50	

	51	Add lines 45 through 50. These are your **total credits**	51	
	52	Subtract line 51 from line 44. If line 51 is more than line 44, enter -0-. . . ▶	52	

Other Taxes	53	Tax on income not effectively connected with a U.S. trade or business from page 4, Schedule NEC, line 15	53	
	54	Self-employment tax. Attach Schedule SE (Form 1040)	54	
	55	Unreported social security and Medicare tax from Form: a ☐ 4137 b ☐ 8919	55	
	56	Additional tax on IRAs, other qualified retirement plans, etc. Attach Form 5329 if required	56	
	57	Transportation tax (see instructions)	57	
	58	a ☐ Schedule H (Form 1040) b ☐ Form 5405, line 16	58	
	59	Add lines 52 through 58. This is your total tax . . . . ▶	59	

Payments	60	Federal income tax withheld from:		
		a Form(s) W-2 or 1099	60a	
		b Form(s) 8805	60b	
		c Form(s) 8288-A	60c	
		d Form(s) 1042-S	60d	
	61	2010 estimated tax payments and amount applied from 2009 return	61	
	62	Additional child tax credit. Attach Form 8812	62	
	63	Amount paid with request for extension to file (see instructions)	63	
	64	Excess social security and tier 1 RRTA tax withheld (see instructions)	64	
	65	Credit for federal tax paid on fuels. Attach Form 4136 . . .	65	
	66	Credits from Form: a ☐ 2439 b ☐ 8839 c ☐ 8801 d ☐ 8885	66	
	67	Credit for amount paid with Form 1040-C	67	
	68	Add lines 60a through 67. These are your **total payments** . . . . . ▶	68	

Refund Direct deposit? See instructions.	69	If line 68 is more than line 59, subtract line 59 from line 68. This is the amount you **overpaid**	69	
	70a	Amount of line 69 you want **refunded to you.** If Form 8888 is attached, check here . ▶ ☐	70a	
	b	Routing number [ ] ▶ c Type: ☐ Checking ☐ Savings		
	d	Account number [ ]		
	e	If you want your refund check mailed to an address outside the United States not shown on page 1, enter it here.		
	71	Amount of line 69 you want **applied to your 2011 estimated tax** ▶	71	

Amount You Owe	72	**Amount you owe.** Subtract line 68 from line 59. For details on how to pay, see instructions ▶	72	
	73	Estimated tax penalty (see instructions)	73	

Third Party Designee	Do you want to allow another person to discuss this return with the IRS (see instructions)? ☐ **Yes.** Complete below. ☐ **No**
	Designee's name ▶ Phone no. ▶ Personal identification number (PIN) ▶ [ ]

Sign Here Keep a copy of this return for your records.	Under penalties of perjury, I declare that I have examined this return and accompanying schedules and statements, and to the best of my knowledge and belief, they are true, correct, and complete. Declaration of preparer (other than taxpayer) is based on all information of which preparer has any knowledge.
	Your signature ▶ Date Your occupation in the United States

Paid Preparer Use Only	Print/Type preparer's name Preparer's signature Date Check ☐ if self-employed PTIN
	Firm's name ▶ Firm's EIN ▶
	Firm's address ▶ Phone no.

Form **1040NR** (2010)

Sample 2 — Continued

Schedule A—Itemized Deductions (See instructions.)   07

State and Local Income Taxes	1	State income taxes	**1**	
	2	Local income taxes	**2**	
	3	Add lines 1 and 2	**3**	
Gifts to U.S. Charities		**Caution:** *If you made a gift and received a benefit in return, see instructions.*		
	4	Gifts by cash or check. If you made any gift of $250 or more, see instructions	**4**	
	5	Other than by cash or check. If you made any gift of $250 or more, see instructions. You **must** attach Form 8283 if the amount of your deduction is over $500 .	**5**	
	6	Carryover from prior year	**6**	
	7	Add lines 4 through 6	**7**	
Casualty and Theft Losses	8	Casualty or theft loss(es). Attach Form 4684. See instructions	**8**	
Job Expenses and Certain Miscellaneous Deductions	9	Unreimbursed employee expenses—job travel, union dues, job education, etc. You **must** attach Form 2106 or Form 2106-EZ if required. See instructions ▶ _____	**9**	
	10	Tax preparation fees	**10**	
	11	Other expenses. See instructions for expenses to deduct here. List type and amount ▶ _____	**11**	
	12	Add lines 9 through 11	**12**	
	13	Enter the amount from Form 1040NR, line 37 . . . . . [**13**]		
	14	Multiply line 13 by 2% (.02)	**14**	
	15	Subtract line 14 from line 12. If line 14 is more than line 12, enter -0-	**15**	
Other Miscellaneous Deductions	16	Other—see instructions for expenses to deduct here. List type and amount ▶	**16**	
Total Itemized Deductions	17	Add the amounts in the far right column for lines 3 through 16. Also enter this amount on Form 1040NR, line 38.	**17**	

Form **1040NR** (2010)

Form 1040NR (2010)

Page **4**

Schedule NEC—Tax on Income Not Effectively Connected With a U.S. Trade or Business (see instructions)

Nature of income		Enter amount of income under the appropriate rate of tax (see instructions)			
		(a) 10%	(b) 15%	(c) 30%	(d) Other (specify)
					% / %
1 Dividends paid by:					
a U.S. corporations	1a				
b Foreign corporations	1b				
2 Interest:					
a Mortgage	2a				
b Paid by foreign corporations	2b				
c Other	2c				
3 Industrial royalties (patents, trademarks, etc.)	3				
4 Motion picture or T.V. copyright royalties	4				
5 Other royalties (copyrights, recording, publishing, etc.)	5				
6 Real property income and natural resources royalties	6				
7 Pensions and annuities	7				
8 Social security benefits	8				
9 Capital gain from line 18 below	9				
10 Gambling—Residents of Canada only. Enter net income in column (c). If zero or less, enter -0-.	10c				
a Winnings					
b Losses					
11 Gambling winnings — Residents of countries other than Canada. Note. Losses not allowed	11				
12 Other (specify) ▶	12				
13 Add lines 1a through 12 in columns (a) through (d)	13				
14 Multiply line 13 by rate of tax at top of each column	14				
15 Tax on income not effectively connected with a U.S. trade or business. Add columns (a) through (d) of line 14. Enter the total here and on Form 1040NR, line 53	15			▶	

Capital Gains and Losses From Sales or Exchanges of Property

16 (a) Kind of property and description (if necessary, attach statement of descriptive details not shown below)	(b) Date acquired (mo., day, yr.)	(c) Date sold (mo., day, yr.)	(d) Sales price	(e) Cost or other basis	(f) LOSS if (e) is more than (d), subtract (d) from (e)	(g) GAIN if (d) is more than (e), subtract (e) from (d)

17 Add columns (f) and (g) of line 16   17 ( )

18 **Capital gain.** Combine columns (f) and (g) of line 17. Enter the net gain here and on line 9 above (if a loss, enter -0-) ▶   18

Enter only the capital gains and losses from property sales or exchanges that are from sources within the United States and not effectively connected with a U.S. business. Do not include a gain or loss on disposing of a U.S. real property interest; report these gains and losses on Schedule D (Form 1040).

Report property sales or exchanges that are effectively connected with a U.S. business on Schedule D (Form 1040), Form 4797, or both.

Form **1040NR** (2010)

Sample 2 — Continued

Schedule OI — Other Information (see instructions)
Answer all questions

A Of what country or countries were you a citizen or national during the tax year? ---

B In what country did you claim residence for tax purposes during the tax year? ---

C Have you ever applied to be a green card holder (lawful permanent resident) of the United States?. . . . . ☐ Yes ☐ No

D Were you ever:
  1. A U.S. citizen?. . . . . ☐ Yes ☐ No
  2. A green card holder (lawful permanent resident) of the United States? . . . . ☐ Yes ☐ No
  If you answer "Yes" to 1 or 2, see Pub. 519, chapter 4, to see expatriation rules that may apply to you.

E If you had a visa on the last day of the tax year, enter your visa type. If you did not have a visa, enter your U.S. immigration status on the last day of the tax year. --

F Have you ever changed your visa type (nonimmigrant status) or U.S. immigration status?. . . . . ☐ Yes ☐ No
  If you answered "Yes," indicate the date and nature of the change. . ▶ --

G List all dates you entered and left the United States during 2010 (see instructions).
  Note. If you are a resident of Canada or Mexico AND commute to work in the United States at frequent intervals, **check the box for Canada or Mexico** and skip to item H . . . . ☐ Canada ☐ Mexico

Date entered United States mm/dd/yy	Date departed United States mm/dd/yy	Date entered United States mm/dd/yy	Date departed United States mm/dd/yy
/ /	/ /	/ /	/ /
/ /	/ /	/ /	/ /
/ /	/ /	/ /	/ /
/ /	/ /	/ /	/ /

H Give number of days (including vacation, nonworkdays, and partial days) you were present in the United States during:
  2008 ----------------------- , 2009 ----------------------- , and 2010 ----------------------- .

I Did you file a U.S. income tax return for any prior year? . . . . ☐ Yes ☐ No
  If "Yes," give the latest year and form number you filed . ▶ --

J Are you filing a return for a trust? . . . . ☐ Yes ☐ No
  If "Yes," did the trust have a U.S. or foreign owner under the grantor trust rules, make a distribution or loan to a U.S. person, or receive a contribution from a U.S. person? . . . . ☐ Yes ☐ No

K Did you receive total compensation of $250,000 or more during the tax year? . . . . ☐ Yes ☐ No
  If "Yes," did you use an alternative method to determine the source of this compensation? . . . . ☐ Yes ☐ No

L Income Exempt from Tax—If you are claiming exemption from income tax under a U.S. income tax treaty with a foreign country, complete 1 and 2 below. See Pub. 901 for more information on tax treaties.
  1. Enter the name of the country, the applicable tax treaty article, the number of months in prior years you claimed the treaty benefit, and the amount of exempt income in the columns below. Attach Form 8833 if required (see instructions).

(a) Country	(b) Tax treaty article	(c) Number of months claimed in prior tax years	(d) Amount of exempt income in current tax year

  (e) Total. Enter this amount on Form 1040NR, line 22. Do not enter it on line 8 or line 12 . . . . |
  2. Were you subject to tax in a foreign country on any of the income shown in 1(d) above? . . . . ☐ Yes ☐ No

Form **1040NR** (2010)

Sample 3
CERTIFICATE OF FOREIGN PERSON'S CLAIM, THAT INCOME IS EFFECTIVELY CONNECTED WITH THE CONDUCT OF A TRADE OR BUSINESS IN THE UNITED STATES (FORM W-8ECI)

Form **W-8ECI** (Rev. February 2006) Department of the Treasury Internal Revenue Service	**Certificate of Foreign Person's Claim That Income Is Effectively Connected With the Conduct of a Trade or Business in the United States** ▶ Section references are to the Internal Revenue Code.　▶ See separate instructions. ▶ Give this form to the withholding agent or payer. Do not send to the IRS.	OMB No. 1545-1621

Note: *Persons submitting this form must file an annual U.S. income tax return to report income claimed to be effectively connected with a U.S. trade or business (see instructions).*

Do not use this form for:	Instead, use Form:
● A beneficial owner solely claiming foreign status or treaty benefits	W-8BEN
● A foreign government, international organization, foreign central bank of issue, foreign tax-exempt organization, foreign private foundation, or government of a U.S. possession claiming the applicability of section(s) 115(2), 501(c), 892, 895, or 1443(b)	W-8EXP

Note: *These entities should use Form W-8ECI if they received effectively connected income (e.g., income from commercial activities).*

● A foreign partnership or a foreign trust (unless claiming an exemption from U.S. withholding on income effectively connected with the conduct of a trade or business in the United States)	W-8BEN or W-8IMY
● A person acting as an intermediary	W-8IMY

Note: *See instructions for additional exceptions.*

Part I　Identification of Beneficial Owner (See instructions.)

1 Name of individual or organization that is the beneficial owner

2 Country of incorporation or organization

3 Type of entity (check the appropriate box): ☐ Individual ☐ Corporation ☐ Disregarded entity
☐ Partnership ☐ Simple trust ☐ Complex trust ☐ Estate
☐ Government ☐ Grantor trust ☐ Central bank of issue ☐ Tax-exempt organization
☐ Private foundation ☐ International organization

4 Permanent residence address (street, apt. or suite no., or rural route). **Do not use a P.O. box.**

City or town, state or province. Include postal code where appropriate.

Country (do not abbreviate)

5 Business address in the United States (street, apt. or suite no., or rural route). **Do not use a P.O. box.**

City or town, state, and ZIP code

6 U.S. taxpayer identification number (required—see instructions) ☐ SSN or ITIN ☐ EIN

7 Foreign tax identifying number, if any (optional)

8 Reference number(s) (see instructions)

9 Specify each item of income that is, or is expected to be, received from the payer that is effectively connected with the conduct of a trade or business in the United States (attach statement if necessary) -----------------------------

Part II　Certification

Under penalties of perjury, I declare that I have examined the information on this form and to the best of my knowledge and belief it is true, correct, and complete. I further certify under penalties of perjury that:

● I am the beneficial owner (or I am authorized to sign for the beneficial owner) of all the income to which this form relates,

● The amounts for which this certification is provided are effectively connected with the conduct of a trade or business in the United States and are includible in my gross income (or the beneficial owner's gross income) for the taxable year, **and**

● The beneficial owner is not a U.S. person.

Furthermore, I authorize this form to be provided to any withholding agent that has control, receipt, or custody of the income of which I am the beneficial owner or any withholding agent that can disburse or make payments of the income of which I am the beneficial owner.

Sign Here

Signature of beneficial owner (or individual authorized to sign for the beneficial owner)　Date (MM-DD-YYYY)　Capacity in which acting

For Paperwork Reduction Act Notice, see separate instructions.　Cat. No. 25045D　Form **W-8ECI** (Rev. 2-2006)

want to check box "h" Other and list Exception #1(b) — Individuals who have opened an interest-bearing bank deposit account that generates income that is effectively connected with their US trade or business or rental property. (See Sample 4.) For more information you can read the instructions, specifically on page 6 to find the above mentioned information, at www.irs.gov/pub/irs-pdf/iw7.pdf.

2.2 Indirect ownership

If you recall from Chapter 2, indirect ownership involves holding the property in an entity such as a corporation, partnership, or trust. The reasons someone would choose indirect ownership over direct ownership are potential asset protection and when people other than husband and wife are owners, it provides a structure and rules for operating your business.

Caution: The US does not generally recognize same-sex and common-law marriages as legal marriages; therefore, if you are not legally married according to US law and operating a business (e.g., rental), you will be deemed to be operating a partnership. You should therefore consider forming a legal partnership and complying with all of the rules of such a partnership.

2.2a Corporation

A corporation is a common way of owning real estate for Canadians; however, if one of your objectives in buying property is either occasional personal use or long-term appreciation, then a corporation is not a good idea.

If you plan to use the property from time to time, you must pay the corporation fair market rent or report as a personal dividend the value of the rent not paid. In both cases, the value of the rent will be subject to double taxation. Because of the double taxation feature of US corporations, very few people create corporations anymore. The reason for the double taxation is that dividends paid to shareholders are not an expense

Sample 4
APPLICATION FOR IRS INDIVIDUAL TAXPAYER IDENTIFICATION NUMBER (FORM W-7)

Form **W-7** (Rev. January 2010) Department of the Treasury Internal Revenue Service

Application for IRS Individual Taxpayer Identification Number
► See instructions.
► For use by individuals who are not U.S. citizens or permanent residents.

OMB No. 1545-0074

An IRS individual taxpayer identification number (ITIN) is for federal tax purposes only.

FOR IRS USE ONLY

Before you begin:

- ***Do not submit*** *this form if you have, or are eligible to get, a U.S. social security number (SSN).*
- *Getting an ITIN does not change your immigration status or your right to work in the United States and does not make you eligible for the earned income credit.*

Reason you are submitting Form W-7. Read the instructions for the box you check. **Caution:** If you check box **b, c, d, e, f,** or **g, you must file a tax return with Form W-7 unless you meet one of the exceptions** (see instructions).

a ☐ Nonresident alien required to get ITIN to claim tax treaty benefit
b ☐ Nonresident alien filing a U.S. tax return
c ☐ U.S. resident alien **(based on days present in the United States)** filing a U.S. tax return
d ☐ Dependent of U.S. citizen/resident alien } Enter name and SSN/ITIN of U.S. citizen/resident alien (see instructions) ►
e ☐ Spouse of U.S. citizen/resident alien
f ☐ Nonresident alien student, professor, or researcher filing a U.S. tax return or claiming an exception
g ☐ Dependent/spouse of a nonresident alien holding a U.S. visa
h ☐ Other (see instructions) ►
Additional information for **a** and **f**: Enter treaty country ► and treaty article number ►

Name (see instructions)
1a First name | Middle name | Last name

Name at birth if different ►
1b First name | Middle name | Last name

Applicant's mailing address
2 Street address, apartment number, or rural route number. **If you have a P.O. box, see page 4.**
City or town, state or province, and country. Include ZIP code or postal code where appropriate.

Foreign (non-U.S.) address (if different from above) (see instructions)
3 Street address, apartment number, or rural route number. **Do not use a P.O. box number.**
City or town, state or province, and country. Include ZIP code or postal code where appropriate.

Birth information
4 Date of birth (month / day / year) / / | Country of birth | City and state or province (optional) | 5 ☐ Male ☐ Female

Other information
6a Country(ies) of citizenship | 6b Foreign tax I.D. number (if any) | 6c Type of U.S. visa (if any), number, and expiration date

6d Identification document(s) submitted (see instructions) ☐ Passport ☐ Driver's license/State I.D.
☐ USCIS documentation ☐ Other
Issued by: No.: Exp. date: / / Entry date in United States / /

6e Have you previously received a U.S. temporary taxpayer identification number (TIN) or employer identification number (EIN)?
☐ **No/Do not know.** Skip line 6f.
☐ **Yes.** Complete line 6f. If more than one, list on a sheet and attach to this form (see instructions).

6f Enter: TIN or EIN ► and
Name under which it was issued ►

6g Name of college/university or company (see instructions)
City and state Length of stay

Sign Here

Under penalties of perjury, I (applicant/delegate/acceptance agent) declare that I have examined this application, including accompanying documentation and statements, and to the best of my knowledge and belief, it is true, correct, and complete. I authorize the IRS to disclose to my acceptance agent returns or return information necessary to resolve matters regarding the assignment of my IRS individual taxpayer identification number (ITIN), including any previously assigned taxpayer identifying number.

Signature of applicant (if delegate, see instructions) | Date (month / day / year) / / | Phone number ( )

Keep a copy for your records.

Name of delegate, if applicable (type or print) | Delegate's relationship to applicant ► | ☐ Parent ☐ Court-appointed guardian ☐ Power of Attorney

Acceptance Agent's Use ONLY

Signature | Date (month / day / year) / / | Phone ( ) Fax ( )
Name and title (type or print) | Name of company | EIN Office Code

For Paperwork Reduction Act Notice, see page 5. Cat. No. 10229L Form **W-7** (Rev. 1-2010)

to the corporation (first level of tax) and, of course, the shareholders pay tax on their individual tax return (second level of tax).

The other reason to avoid corporate tax (as if double tax were not enough), is that all income is taxed at ordinary income tax rates. In other words, you miss out on the lower capital gains tax rate. Currently the highest ordinary income tax rate is 35 percent, whereas the capital gains tax is a flat rate of 15 percent, with few exceptions.

2.2b Partnership

In the US a partnership comes in many different flavors. We have a traditional General Partnership (GP), Limited Partnership (LP), Limited Liability Partnership (LLP), Limited Liability Limited Partnership (LLLP), and Limited Liability Company (LLC). While an LLC is not technically a partnership, it behaves very similarly to an LLP. However, Canadians should care about one difference in particular, as it relates to how the LLC is treated in Canada.

In the US, a partnership is not a taxable entity, but partners must file a tax return to report the activity and issue a Schedule K-1: Partner's Share of Income, Deductions, Credits, etc., which is a form used to report each partner's share of the income, expenses, and profits. The Schedule K-1 (see Sample 5) is the document to be given to your tax preparer. All of the income, expenses, and profits flow down to the partners and the partners report the profits on their individual income tax returns. From a tax perspective, the individual will be required to file tax returns, the same as if the property was owned directly. Canada views an LLC as a corporation, which leads to a mismatch of foreign tax credits. Bottom line is that you will be paying taxes in both countries without the availability of foreign tax credits to offset the tax in Canada.

A partnership that has "effectively connected taxable income" (e.g., rental income allocable to foreign partners) must

Sample 5
SCHEDULE K-1: PARTNER'S SHARE OF INCOME, DEDUCTIONS, CREDITS, ETC. (FORM 1065)

651110

☐ Final K-1   ☐ Amended K-1   OMB No. 1545-0099

Schedule K-1
(Form 1065)
2010

Department of the Treasury
Internal Revenue Service

For calendar year 2010, or tax
year beginning _____ , 2010
ending _____ , 20 _____

**Partner's Share of Income, Deductions,
Credits, etc.**
► See back of form and separate instructions.

Part I — Information About the Partnership

A Partnership's employer identification number

B Partnership's name, address, city, state, and ZIP code

C IRS Center where partnership filed return

D ☐ Check if this is a publicly traded partnership (PTP)

Part II — Information About the Partner

E Partner's identifying number

F Partner's name, address, city, state, and ZIP code

G ☐ General partner or LLC member-manager   ☐ Limited partner or other LLC member

H ☐ Domestic partner   ☐ Foreign partner

I What type of entity is this partner? _____

J Partner's share of profit, loss, and capital (see instructions):

	Beginning	Ending
Profit	%	%
Loss	%	%
Capital	%	%

K Partner's share of liabilities at year end:

Nonrecourse . . . . $ _____
Qualified nonrecourse financing . $ _____
Recourse . . . . $ _____

L Partner's capital account analysis:

Beginning capital account . . . $ _____
Capital contributed during the year $ _____
Current year increase (decrease) . $ _____
Withdrawals & distributions . . $ (_____)
Ending capital account . . . . $ _____

☐ Tax basis   ☐ GAAP   ☐ Section 704(b) book
☐ Other (explain)

M Did the partner contribute property with a built-in gain or loss?
☐ Yes   ☐ No
If "Yes", attach statement (see instructions)

Part III — Partner's Share of Current Year Income, Deductions, Credits, and Other Items

1 Ordinary business income (loss)	**15** Credits	
2 Net rental real estate income (loss)		
3 Other net rental income (loss)	**16** Foreign transactions	
4 Guaranteed payments		
5 Interest income		
6a Ordinary dividends		
6b Qualified dividends		
7 Royalties		
8 Net short-term capital gain (loss)		
9a Net long-term capital gain (loss)	**17** Alternative minimum tax (AMT) items	
9b Collectibles (28%) gain (loss)		
9c Unrecaptured section 1250 gain		
10 Net section 1231 gain (loss)	**18** Tax-exempt income and nondeductible expenses	
11 Other income (loss)		
	19 Distributions	
12 Section 179 deduction		
13 Other deductions	**20** Other information	
14 Self-employment earnings (loss)		

*See attached statement for additional information.

For IRS Use Only

For Paperwork Reduction Act Notice, see Instructions for Form 1065.   Cat. No. 11394R   Schedule K-1 (Form 1065) 2010

Schedule K-1 (Form 1065) 2010   Page **2**

This list identifies the codes used on Schedule K-1 for all partners and provides summarized reporting information for partners who file Form 1040.
For detailed reporting and filing information, see the separate Partner's Instructions for Schedule K-1 and the instructions for your income tax return.

1. Ordinary business income (loss). Determine whether the income (loss) is passive or nonpassive and enter on your return as follows.

	Report on
Passive loss	See the Partner's Instructions
Passive income	Schedule E, line 28, column (g)
Nonpassive loss	Schedule E, line 28, column (h)
Nonpassive income	Schedule E, line 28, column (j)

2. Net rental real estate income (loss)   See the Partner's Instructions

3. Other net rental income (loss)

Net income	Schedule E, line 28, column (g)
Net loss	See the Partner's Instructions

4. Guaranteed payments   Schedule E, line 28, column (j)
5. Interest income   Form 1040, line 8a
6a. Ordinary dividends   Form 1040, line 9a
6b. Qualified dividends   Form 1040, line 9b
7. Royalties   Schedule E, line 4
8. Net short-term capital gain (loss)   Schedule D, line 5, column (f)
9a. Net long-term capital gain (loss)   Schedule D, line 12, column (f)
9b. Collectibles (28%) gain (loss)   28% Rate Gain Worksheet, line 4 (Schedule D instructions)
9c. Unrecaptured section 1250 gain   See the Partner's Instructions
10. Net section 1231 gain (loss)   See the Partner's Instructions
11. Other income (loss)

	Code	
A	Other portfolio income (loss)	See the Partner's Instructions
B	Involuntary conversions	See the Partner's Instructions
C	Sec. 1256 contracts & straddles	Form 6781, line 1
D	Mining exploration costs recapture	See Pub. 535
E	Cancellation of debt	Form 1040, line 21 or Form 982
F	Other income (loss)	See the Partner's Instructions

12. Section 179 deduction   See the Partner's Instructions
13. Other deductions

A	Cash contributions (50%)	
B	Cash contributions (30%)	
C	Noncash contributions (50%)	
D	Noncash contributions (30%)	See the Partner's
E	Capital gain property to a 50% organization (30%)	Instructions
F	Capital gain property (20%)	
G	Contributions (100%)	
H	Investment interest expense	Form 4952, line 1
I	Deductions—royalty income	Schedule E, line 18
J	Section 59(e)(2) expenditures	See the Partner's Instructions
K	Deductions—portfolio (2% floor)	Schedule A, line 23
L	Deductions—portfolio (other)	Schedule A, line 28
M	Amounts paid for medical insurance	Schedule A, line 1 or Form 1040, line 29
N	Educational assistance benefits	See the Partner's Instructions
O	Dependent care benefits	Form 2441, line 12
P	Preproductive period expenses	See the Partner's Instructions
Q	Commercial revitalization deduction from rental real estate activities	See Form 8582 instructions
R	Pensions and IRAs	See the Partner's Instructions
S	Reforestation expense deduction	See the Partner's Instructions
T	Domestic production activities information	See Form 8903 instructions
U	Qualified production activities income	Form 8903, line 7b
V	Employer's Form W-2 wages	Form 8903, line 17
W	Other deductions	See the Partner's Instructions

14. Self-employment earnings (loss)

Note. *If you have a section 179 deduction or any partner-level deductions, see the Partner's Instructions before completing Schedule SE.*

A	Net earnings (loss) from self-employment	Schedule SE, Section A or B
B	Gross farming or fishing income	See the Partner's Instructions
C	Gross non-farm income	See the Partner's Instructions

15. Credits

A	Low-income housing credit (section 42(j)(5)) from pre-2008 buildings	See the Partner's Instructions
B	Low-income housing credit (other) from pre-2008 buildings	See the Partner's Instructions
C	Low-income housing credit (section 42(j)(5)) from post-2007 buildings	Form 8586, line 11
D	Low-income housing credit (other) from post-2007 buildings	Form 8586, line 11
E	Qualified rehabilitation expenditures (rental real estate)	
F	Other rental real estate credits	See the Partner's Instructions
G	Other rental credits	
H	Undistributed capital gains credit	Form 1040, line 71; check box a
I	Alcohol and cellulosic biofuels credit	Form 6478, line 8
J	Work opportunity credit	Form 5884, line 3

	Code	Report on
K	Disabled access credit	See the Partner's Instructions
L	Empowerment zone and renewal community employment credit	Form 8844, line 3
M	Credit for increasing research activities	See the Partner's Instructions
N	Credit for employer social security and Medicare taxes	Form 8846, line 5
O	Backup withholding	Form 1040, line 61
P	Other credits	See the Partner's Instructions

16. Foreign transactions

A	Name of country or U.S. possession	
B	Gross income from all sources	Form 1116, Part I
C	Gross income sourced at partner level	

Foreign gross income sourced at partnership level

D	Passive category	
E	General category	Form 1116, Part I
F	Other	

Deductions allocated and apportioned at partner level

G	Interest expense	Form 1116, Part I
H	Other	Form 1116, Part I

Deductions allocated and apportioned at partnership level to foreign source income

I	Passive category	
J	General category	Form 1116, Part I
K	Other	

Other information

L	Total foreign taxes paid	Form 1116, Part II
M	Total foreign taxes accrued	Form 1116, Part II
N	Reduction in taxes available for credit	Form 1116, line 12
O	Foreign trading gross receipts	Form 8873
P	Extraterritorial income exclusion	Form 8873
Q	Other foreign transactions	See the Partner's Instructions

17. Alternative minimum tax (AMT) items

A	Post-1986 depreciation adjustment	
B	Adjusted gain or loss	See the Partner's
C	Depletion (other than oil & gas)	Instructions and
D	Oil, gas, & geothermal—gross income	the Instructions for
E	Oil, gas, & geothermal—deductions	Form 6251
F	Other AMT items	

18. Tax-exempt income and nondeductible expenses

A	Tax-exempt interest income	Form 1040, line 8b
B	Other tax-exempt income	See the Partner's Instructions
C	Nondeductible expenses	See the Partner's Instructions

19. Distributions

A	Cash and marketable securities	
B	Distribution subject to section 737	See the Partner's Instructions
C	Other property	

20. Other information

A	Investment income	Form 4952, line 4a
B	Investment expenses	Form 4952, line 5
C	Fuel tax credit information	Form 4136
D	Qualified rehabilitation expenditures (other than rental real estate)	See the Partner's Instructions
E	Basis of energy property	See the Partner's Instructions
F	Recapture of low-income housing credit (section 42(j)(5))	Form 8611, line 8
G	Recapture of low-income housing credit (other)	Form 8611, line 8
H	Recapture of investment credit	See Form 4255
I	Recapture of other credits	See the Partner's Instructions
J	Look-back interest—completed long-term contracts	See Form 8697
K	Look-back interest—income forecast method	See Form 8866
L	Dispositions of property with section 179 deductions	
M	Recapture of section 179 deduction	
N	Interest expense for corporate partners	
O	Section 453(l)(3) information	
P	Section 453A(c) information	
Q	Section 1260(b) information	
R	Interest allocable to production expenditures	See the Partner's
S	CCF nonqualified withdrawals	Instructions
T	Depletion information—oil and gas	
U	Amortization of reforestation costs	
V	Unrelated business taxable income	
W	Precontribution gain (loss)	
X	Section 108(i) information	
Y	Other information	

make withholding tax payments. Those payments are made using Annual Return for Partnership Withholding Tax (Form 8804), Foreign Partner's Information Statement of Section 1446 Withholding Tax (Form 8805), and Partnership Withholding Tax Payment Voucher (Form 8813). (See Samples 6, 7, and 8.)

If a Canadian resident owns a US LLC there is no requirement to file a Canadian corporate return unless that LLC is doing business in Canada. The individual may have to file (with Canada Revenue Agency) a Foreign Income Verification Statement (Form T1135) to indicate he or she has in excess of $100,000 (Canadian) of assets outside Canada, but would not have to report if it was personal-use property. As an example, if an individual has a condo he or she is using for his or her personal use, and it was in excess of $100,000 (Canadian), he or she would not have to report it. If he or she was renting out the condo, he or she would have to report it. (See Sample 9.)

2.2c Trust

Trusts in the US are different from those in Canada. The most common type of trust in the US is a revocable living trust. There are three features that make this type of trust unique from Canadian trusts:

➤ The trust is revocable.

➤ The trust is established by the individual for the benefit of the individual.

➤ The trust pays no tax.

When a trust is revocable, it means, as the name implies, that the individual can revoke it at any time. Traditionally, trusts are irrevocable, which means once established there is no turning back; this is how most trusts in Canada are formed. In general, an individual with an irrevocable trust can have no rights or control over the trust once established. The money put into the trust is considered gifted away. In the US, the revocable living trust is treated as if the trust did not exist for

ANNUAL RETURN FOR PARTNERSHIP WITHHOLDING TAX (FORM 8804)

Form **8804**	**Annual Return for Partnership Withholding Tax (Section 1446)**	OMB No. 1545-1119
	▶ See separate Instructions for Forms 8804, 8805, and 8813.	
	▶ Attach Form(s) 8804-C and 8805.	20**10**
Department of the Treasury Internal Revenue Service	For calendar year 2010 or tax year beginning ____ , 2010, and ending ____ , 20 ____	

Check this box if the partnership keeps its records and books of account outside the United States and Puerto Rico . . . ▶ ☐

Part I Partnership

1a Name of partnership	b U.S. employer identification number		
c Number, street, and room or suite no. If a P.O. box, see instructions.	**For IRS Use Only**		
	CC		FD
	RD		FF
d City, state, and ZIP code. If a foreign address, see instructions.	CAF		FP
	CR		I
	EDC		

Part II Withholding Agent

2a Name of withholding agent. If partnership is also the withholding agent, enter "SAME" and do not complete lines 2b, 2c, or 2d.	b Withholding agent's U.S. employer identification number
c Number, street, and room or suite no. If a P.O. box, see instructions.	
d City, state, and ZIP code	

Part III Section 1446 Tax Liability and Payments

3a	Enter number of foreign partners . . . . ▶	--------		
b	Enter number of Forms 8805 attached to this Form 8804 . . ▶	--------		
c	Enter number of Forms 8804-C attached to Forms 8805 . . . ▶	--------		
4	Total effectively connected taxable income allocable to foreign partners (see instructions):			
a	Net ordinary income and net short-term capital gain	4a		
b	Reduction to line 4a for state and local taxes under Regulations section 1.1446-6(c)(1)(iii)	4b (	)	
c	Reduction to line 4a for certified foreign partner-level items submitted using Form 8804-C	4c (	)	
d	Combine lines 4a, 4b, and 4c			4d
e	28% rate gain allocable to non-corporate partners	4e		
f	Reduction to line 4e for state and local taxes under Regulations section 1.1446-6(c)(1)(iii)	4f (	)	
g	Reduction to line 4e for certified foreign partner-level items submitted using Form 8804-C	4g (	)	
h	Combine lines 4e, 4f, and 4g			4h
i	Unrecaptured section 1250 gain allocable to non-corporate partners	4i		
j	Reduction to line 4i for state and local taxes under Regulations section 1.1446-6(c)(1)(iii)	4j (	)	
k	Reduction to line 4i for certified foreign partner-level items submitted using Form 8804-C	4k (	)	
l	Combine lines 4i, 4j, and 4k			4l
m	Qualified dividend income and net long-term capital gain (including net section 1231 gain) allocable to non-corporate partners . .	4m		
n	Reduction to line 4m for state and local taxes under Regulations section 1.1446-6(c)(1)(iii)	4n (	)	
o	Reduction to line 4m for certified foreign partner-level items submitted using Form 8804-C	4o (	)	
p	Combine lines 4m, 4n, and 4o			4p

For Paperwork Reduction Act Notice, see separate instructions for Forms 8804, 8805, and 8813.   Cat. No. 10077T   Form **8804** (2010)

Sample 6 — Continued

5	Gross section 1446 tax liability:			
a	Multiply line 4d by 35% (.35)	5a		
b	Multiply line 4h by 28% (.28)	5b		
c	Multiply line 4l by 25% (.25)	5c		
d	Multiply line 4p by 15% (.15)	5d		
e	Add lines 5a through 5d		5e	

6a	Payments of section 1446 tax made by the partnership identified on line 1a during its tax year (or with a request for an extension of time to file) and amount credited from 2009 Form 8804	6a	
b	Section 1446 tax paid or withheld by another partnership in which the partnership identified on line 1a was a partner during the tax year (attach Form(s) 1042-S or 8805)	6b	
c	Section 1445(a) or 1445(e)(1) tax withheld from or paid by the partnership identified on line 1a during the tax year for a disposition of a U.S. real property interest. Attach Form(s) 1042-S or 8288-A. See the instructions	6c	

7	**Total payments.** Add lines 6a through 6c	7	
8	Estimated tax penalty (see instructions). Check if Schedule A (Form 8804) is attached . . ☐	8	
9	Add lines 5e and 8	9	
10	**Balance due.** If line 7 is smaller than line 9, enter balance due. Attach a check or money order for the full amount payable to the "United States Treasury." Write the partnership's U.S. employer identification number, tax year, and Form 8804 on it	10	
11	**Overpayment.** If line 7 is more than line 9, enter amount overpaid	11	
12	Amount of line 11 you want **refunded to you** . . . . ▶	12	
13	Amount of line 11 you want **credited to next year's Form 8804** . . | 13 |		

Sign Here

Under penalties of perjury, I declare that I have examined this return, including accompanying schedules and statements, and to the best of my knowledge and belief, it is true, correct, and complete. Declaration of preparer (other than general partner, limited liability company member, or withholding agent) is based on all information of which preparer has any knowledge.

▶ _____
Signature of general partner, limited liability company member, or withholding agent　　Title　　Date

Paid Preparer Use Only	Print/Type preparer's name	Preparer's signature	Date	Check ☐ if self-employed	PTIN
	Firm's name ▶			Firm's EIN ▶	
	Firm's address ▶			Phone no.	

Form **8804** (2010)

FOREIGN PARTNER'S INFORMATION STATEMENT OF SECTION 1446 WITHHOLDING TAX (FORM 8805)

Form **8805**	**Foreign Partner's Information Statement of Section 1446 Withholding Tax**	OMB No. 1545-1119
Department of the Treasury Internal Revenue Service	▶ See separate Instructions for Forms 8804, 8805, and 8813. For partnership's calendar year 2010, or tax year beginning _____ , 2010. and ending _____ , 20	**2010** Copy A for Internal Revenue Service Attach to Form 8804.

1a Foreign partner's name	b U.S. identifying number	5a Name of partnership	b U.S. EIN
c Address (if a foreign address, see instructions)		c Address (if a foreign address, see instructions)	
2 Account number assigned by partnership (if any)		6 Withholding agent's name. If partnership is also the withholding agent, enter "SAME" and do not complete line 7.	
3 Type of partner (specify—see instructions) ▶			
4 Country code of partner (enter two-letter code; see instructions)		7 Withholding agent's U.S. employer identification number	

8a	Check if the partnership identified on line 5a owns an interest in one or more partnerships	☐
b	Check if any of the partnership's effectively connected taxable income (ECTI) is exempt from U.S. tax for the partner identified on line 1a	☐
9	Partnership's ECTI allocable to partner for the tax year (see instructions)	**9**
10	Total tax credit allowed to partner under section 1446 (see instructions). **Individual and corporate partners:** Claim this amount as a credit against your U.S. income tax on Form 1040NR, 1120-F, etc.	**10**

Schedule T—Beneficiary Information (see instructions)

11a Name of beneficiary	c Address (if a foreign address, see instructions)
b U.S. identifying number of beneficiary	

12	Amount of ECTI on line 9 to be included in the beneficiary's gross income (see instructions)	**12**
13	Amount of tax credit on line 10 that the beneficiary is entitled to claim on its return (see instructions) . .	**13**

For Paperwork Reduction Act Notice, see separate Instructions for Forms 8804, 8805, and 8813.   Cat. No. 10078E   Form **8805** (2010)

Sample 8
PARTNERSHIP WITHHOLDING TAX PAYMENT VOUCHER (FORM 8813)

Form **8813**	Partnership Withholding Tax Payment Voucher (Section 1446)	
(Rev. December 2008)	▶ See separate Instructions for Forms 8804, 8805, and 8813.	OMB No. 1545-1119
Department of the Treasury Internal Revenue Service	For calendar year _____, or tax year beginning _____, 20___, and ending _____, 20___	

Mail this voucher with a check or money order payable to the "United States Treasury." Write the partnership's employer identification number, tax year, and "Form 8813" on the check or money order.	**1** Partnership's U.S. employer identification number	**2** Amount of this payment $
	3 PARTNERSHIP'S name, address, (number, street, and room or suite no.), city, state, and ZIP code. If a P.O. box or foreign address, see instructions.	

▶ **Do not staple or attach this voucher to your payment.**

▶ **Do not send cash.**

▶ **If you have applied the provisions of Regulations section 1.1446-6, attach all required Forms 8804-C and computations (see instructions).**

For Paperwork Reduction Act Notice, see separate Instructions for Forms 8804, 8805, and 8813.   Cat. No. 10681H   Form **8813** (Rev. 12-2008)

Sample 9
FOREIGN INCOME VERIFICATION STATEMENT (FORM T1135)

Canada Revenue Agency / **Agence du revenu du Canada**

For departmental use

FOREIGN INCOME VERIFICATION STATEMENT

Complete and file this statement with your tax return (or, if a partnership, with your partnership information return) if at any time in the year the total cost amount of all specified foreign property you owned or held a beneficial interest in was more than $100,000.

Identification

Check (✓) a box to indicate who you are reporting for, and complete the areas that apply.

☐ individual — First name / Last name / Initial / Social insurance number

☐ corporation — Corporation's name / Business Number (BN) ... R C

☐ trust — Trust's name / Account number T – –

☐ partnership — Partnership's name / Partnership's identification number

Reporting taxpayer's address

No. Street — Postal code

City — Province or territory

For what tax year are you filing this statement? | | | | or From | Year Month Day | To | Year Month Day |

Type of Property (It is important that you see the attached instructions for details on the types of property that must be reported).	For each type of property that applies to you, indicate the total cost of the investment by checking (✓) the appropriate box					
	+ $1 Million	+ $700,000	+ $500,000	+ $300,000	+ $100,000	Less than $100,000
1. Funds held outside Canada	☐	☐	☐	☐	☐	☐
2. Shares of non-resident corporations, other than foreign affiliates	☐	☐	☐	☐	☐	☐
3. Indebtedness owed by non-residents	☐	☐	☐	☐	☐	☐
4. Interests in non-resident trusts	☐	☐	☐	☐	☐	☐
5. Real property outside Canada	☐	☐	☐	☐	☐	☐
6. Other property outside Canada	☐	☐	☐	☐	☐	☐

Where are the above investments located? (Check appropriate box(es)) United States ☐ U.K. ☐ Europe, other than U.K. ☐ Southeast Asia ☐ Caribbean ☐ Other ☐

Total income reported on your tax return in the year from the above assets $ _____ 00

Certification

I certify that the information given on this statement is, to my knowledge, correct and complete, and fully discloses the reporting taxpayer's specified foreign property and related foreign income.

Print name _____

Sign here

It is a serious offence to file a false statement.

_____ Position or title

Telephone ( ) — Date _____

If you were paid to prepare this statement, provide the following information:

Your name _____
Address _____
_____
_____
Postal code _____
Telephone ( )

T1135 E (07) — (Ce formulaire existe en français.) — 3774 — **Canada** income tax purposes, so not only does the trust pay no income tax, it does not even file a tax return.

Trusts in Canada generally have a deemed disposition of the assets within the trust every 21 years. This means that the trust is deemed to dispose of and reacquire certain types of property in the trust every 21 years. The 21-year rule prevents the allocation of income and gains arising from the deemed sale to beneficiaries, which means the entire amount (gains included) will be taxed at the top marginal tax rate. Also, since the assets in the trust have not actually been sold, there will be a shortage of cash to pay the tax due.

While irrevocable trusts exist in the US, revocable trusts are more common; in Canada, the irrevocable trust is used. Canada does not have anything that is exactly like a US revocable living trust.

In the US, people use revocable trusts primarily to avoid probate fees (discussed in Chapter 4). As I mentioned earlier, avoiding probate can be done in a couple of different ways that does not cost any money, so in most cases a revocable living trust is not necessary for Canadians buying real estate in the US. Few people use Canadian trusts to purchase US real estate because they have to gift the money away in order to do so.

There is one type of trust that could be beneficial in the right circumstances, and that trust is called The Cross Border Trust[SM]. The trust was developed by David Altro, an attorney in Montreal. This trust is suited for second homes with a value of at least $750,000 USD. The trust provides many of the best features of US and Canadian trusts, but avoids the pitfalls.

My recommendation is to avoid trusts unless you decide either the US revocable living trust or The Cross Border Trust is appropriate for your circumstances; corporations and partnerships are generally much better choices. For a typical investor, owning the property directly or using a US limited liability partnership are the best choices.

3. Selling the Property

In the US, capital gains are broken down into short-term and long-term gains. A long-term gain is defined as a gain with a holding period of at least one year and a day; all other gains are defined as short-term. The reason for the distinction is that long-term gains have favorable tax treatment. Currently, the tax rate on long-term gains is a flat 15 percent federal tax, with some exceptions. An additional state income tax may be applicable. (Section **4.** discusses state income taxes.) Short-term gains are taxed as ordinary income, subject to the progressive tax-rate system. At the lowest levels the marginal rate is 10 percent, and at the highest, 35 percent.

As a nonresident alien selling real estate in the US, you will be subject to the Foreign Investment Real Property Tax Act (FIRPTA). FIRPTA states that barring an exception, the nonresident will be required to pay a 10 percent withholding tax on the gross proceeds of the real estate. The withholding would be required even if you had a loss on the sale of the property. The two most common exceptions are:

1. The buyer purchases the home for $300,000 or less and intends to occupy the property. By this the IRS means there must be a definite plan to reside at the property at least 50 percent of the number of days the property is used by any person during the first two years. When counting the number of days the property is used, do not count the days the property is vacant.

2. Where the purchaser receives a statement from the seller stating that the seller is not a foreign person. This could be true if a US entity is the owner of the property.

To the extent withholding is required, the amount of withholding may be reduced below 10 percent of the gross sale price when the IRS certifies that a reduced amount applies. Such a certification is permitted only if the seller applies to the IRS for reduced withholding by filing an Application for Withholding Certificate for Dispositions by Foreign Persons of US

Real Property Interests (Form 8288-B) no later than the closing date of the sale. (See Sample 10.) The IRS will specify the amount of withholding required.

In most cases you will want to file Form 8288-B so that you are not giving an interest-free loan to the government. For example, say you bought a home for $80,000 and sold it for $100,000. Your ultimate federal tax liability will be 15 percent on the $20,000 gain, or $3,000. If you do not file the form, 10 percent of $100,000 or $10,000 with be withheld, an overpayment of $7,000. Sure you will receive a refund of the difference when you file your tax return, but if you sold the property in January 2011, you may not get your money back until February or March of 2012, which is a 13- to 14-month interest-free loan to the government.

Caution: The IRS typically takes 8 weeks but can take up to 12 weeks or more to return the withholding certificate. Send in Form 8288-B as soon as you can and when possible, make sure the closing date is far enough away to allow time for the IRS to process and return the certificate in time for the closing.

3.1 Foreign tax credits

Given that two or more countries may want to tax the same income, there needs to be a way to avoid paying tax on the same income more than once; there are two basic ways this can happen. The first way is through tax treaties that specify which country gets to tax what income. The second way is through foreign tax credits. Because we are talking about real property, both countries have the right to tax the gains, but if we were talking about gains on a US portfolio, the treaty specifies that the gain is taxed only in the country of residence; Canada in this case. However, since the gain is from the sale of real property, the only option available is to take a credit (a dollar-for-dollar reduction in your tax) on your Canadian return. For individuals, the foreign tax credit is calculated on IRS Form 1116. (See Sample 11.)

Sample 10
APPLICATION FOR WITHHOLDING CERTIFICATE FOR DISPOSITIONS BY FOREIGN PERSONS OF US REAL PROPERTY INTERESTS (FORM 8288-B)

Form **8288-B** (Rev. November 2006) Department of the Treasury Internal Revenue Service	**Application for Withholding Certificate for Dispositions by Foreign Persons of U.S. Real Property Interests** ▶ Please type or print.	OMB No. 1545-1060

1 Name of transferor (attach additional sheets if more than one transferor) | **Identification number**

Street address, apt. or suite no., or rural route. Do not use a P.O. box.

City, state or province, and country (if not U.S.). Include ZIP code or postal code where appropriate.

2 Name of transferee (attach additional sheets if more than one transferee) | **Identification number**

Street address, apt. or suite no., or rural route. Do not use a P.O. box.

City, state or province, and country (if not U.S.). Include ZIP code or postal code where appropriate.

3 Applicant is: Transferor ☐   Transferee ☐

4a Name of withholding agent (see instructions) | **b Identification number**

c Name of estate, trust, or entity (if applicable) | **d Identification number**

5 Address where you want withholding certificate sent (street address, apt. or suite no., P.O. box, or rural route number) | Phone number (optional) (   )

City, state or province, and country (if not U.S.). Include ZIP code or postal code where appropriate.

6 Description of U.S. real property transaction:
a Date of transfer (month, day, year) (see inst.) ....   **b** Contract price $ ....
c Type of interest transferred: ☐ Real property   ☐ Associated personal property
                                    ☐ Domestic U.S. real property holding corporation
d Use of property at time of sale: ☐ Rental or commercial   ☐ Personal   ☐ Other (attach explanation)
e Adjusted basis $ ....
f Location and general description of property (for a real property interest), description (for associated personal property), or the class or type and amount of the interest (for an interest in a U.S. real property holding corporation). See instructions.

----

g For the 3 preceding tax years:
  (1) Were U.S. income tax returns filed relating to the U.S. real property interest? . . . . ☐ Yes   ☐ No
  If "Yes," when and where were those returns filed? ▶ _____

  (2) Were U.S. income taxes paid relating to the U.S. real property interest? . . . . ☐ Yes   ☐ No
  If "Yes," enter the amount of tax paid for each year ▶ _____

7 Check the box to indicate the reason a withholding certificate should be issued. See the instructions for information that must be attached to Form 8288-B.
a ☐ The transferor is exempt from U.S. tax or nonrecognition treatment applies.
b ☐ The transferor's maximum tax liability is less than the tax required to be withheld.
c ☐ The special installment sales rules described in section 7 of Rev. Proc. 2000-35 allow reduced withholding.
8 Does the transferor have any unsatisfied withholding liability under section 1445? . . . . ☐ Yes   ☐ No
See the instructions for information required to be attached.
9 Is this application for a withholding certificate made under section 1445(e)? . . . . ☐ Yes   ☐ No
If "Yes," check the applicable box in **a** and the applicable box in **b** below.
a Type of transaction: ☐ 1445(e)(1) ☐ 1445(e)(2) ☐ 1445(e)(3) ☐ 1445(e)(5) ☐ 1445(e)(6)
b Applicant is: ☐ Taxpayer   ☐ Other person required to withhold. Specify your title (e.g., trustee) ▶ _____

Under penalties of perjury, I declare that I have examined this application and accompanying attachments, and, to the best of my knowledge and belief, they are true, correct, and complete.

Signature	Title (if applicable)	Date

For Privacy Act and Paperwork Reduction Act Notice, see the instructions.   Cat. No. 10128Z   Form **8288-B** (Rev. 11-2006)

Sample 11
FOREIGN TAX CREDIT (FORM 1116)

Form **1116**	**Foreign Tax Credit**	OMB No. 1545-0121
Department of the Treasury Internal Revenue Service (99)	(Individual, Estate, or Trust) ► Attach to Form 1040, 1040NR, 1041, or 990-T. ► See separate instructions.	20**10** Attachment Sequence No. **19**

Name | Identifying number as shown on page 1 of your tax return

Use a separate Form 1116 for each category of income listed below. See **Categories of Income** in the instructions. Check only one box on each Form 1116. Report all amounts in U.S. dollars except where specified in Part II below.

a ☐ Passive category income   c ☐ Section 901(j) income   e ☐ Lump-sum distributions

b ☐ General category income   d ☐ Certain income re-sourced by treaty

f Resident of (name of country) ►

Note: *If you paid taxes to only one foreign country or U.S. possession, use column A in Part I and line A in Part II. If you paid taxes to more than one foreign country or U.S. possession, use a separate column and line for each country or possession.*

Part I   Taxable Income or Loss From Sources Outside the United States (for Category Checked Above)

		Foreign Country or U.S. Possession			Total (Add cols. A, B, and C.)
		A	**B**	**C**	
g	Enter the name of the foreign country or U.S. possession . . . . ►				
1a	Gross income from sources within country shown above and of the type checked above (see instructions): _____ _____ _____				1a
b	Check if line 1a is compensation for personal services as an employee, your total compensation from all sources is $250,000 or more, and you used an alternative basis to determine its source (see instructions) . . ► ☐				
Deductions and losses (Caution: See instructions):					
2	Expenses **definitely related** to the income on line 1a (attach statement)				
3	Pro rata share of other deductions **not definitely related:**				
a	Certain itemized deductions or standard deduction (see instructions)				
b	Other deductions (attach statement)				
c	Add lines 3a and 3b				
d	Gross foreign source income (see instructions) .				
e	Gross income from all sources (see instructions) .				
f	Divide line 3d by line 3e (see instructions) . . .				
g	Multiply line 3c by line 3f				
4	Pro rata share of interest expense (see instructions):				
a	Home mortgage interest (use worksheet on page 14 of the instructions)				
b	Other interest expense				
5	Losses from foreign sources				
6	Add lines 2, 3g, 4a, 4b, and 5				6
7	Subtract line 6 from line 1a. Enter the result here and on line 14, page 2 . . . . ►				7

Part II   Foreign Taxes Paid or Accrued (see instructions)

Country	Credit is claimed for taxes (you must check one)		Foreign taxes paid or accrued								
	(h) ☐ Paid		In foreign currency				In U.S. dollars				
	(i) ☐ Accrued		Taxes withheld at source on:			(n) Other foreign taxes paid or accrued	Taxes withheld at source on:			(r) Other foreign taxes paid or accrued	(s) Total foreign taxes paid or accrued (add cols. (o) through (r))
	(j) Date paid or accrued	(k) Dividends	(l) Rents and royalties	(m) Interest			(o) Dividends	(p) Rents and royalties	(q) Interest		
A											
B											
C											
8	Add lines A through C, column (s). Enter the total here and on line 9, page 2 . . . . ►									8	

For Paperwork Reduction Act Notice, see instructions.   Cat. No. 11440U   Form **1116** (2010)

Sample 11— Continued

Part III Figuring the Credit

9	Enter the amount from line 8. These are your total foreign taxes paid or accrued for the category of income checked above Part I . .	9	
10	Carryback or carryover (attach detailed computation)	10	
11	Add lines 9 and 10	11	
12	Reduction in foreign taxes (see instructions)	12	
13	Subtract line 12 from line 11. This is the total amount of foreign taxes available for credit (see instructions)		13
14	Enter the amount from line 7. This is your taxable income or (loss) from sources outside the United States (before adjustments) for the category of income checked above Part I (see instructions)	14	
15	Adjustments to line 14 (see instructions)	15	
16	Combine the amounts on lines 14 and 15. This is your net foreign source taxable income. (If the result is zero or less, you have no foreign tax credit for the category of income you checked above Part I. Skip lines 17 through 21. However, if you are filing more than one Form 1116, you must complete line 19.)	16	
17	**Individuals:** Enter the amount from Form 1040, line 41, or Form 1040NR, line 39. **Estates and trusts:** Enter your taxable income without the deduction for your exemption	17	
	Caution: *If you figured your tax using the lower rates on qualified dividends or capital gains, see instructions.*		
18	Divide line 16 by line 17. If line 16 is more than line 17, enter "1"		18
19	**Individuals:** Enter the amount from Form 1040, line 44. If you are a nonresident alien, enter the amount from Form 1040NR, line 42. **Estates and trusts:** Enter the amount from Form 1041, Schedule G, line 1a, or the total of Form 990-T, lines 36 and 37		19
	Caution: *If you are completing line 19 for separate category e (lump-sum distributions), see instructions.*		
20	Multiply line 19 by line 18 (maximum amount of credit)		20
21	Enter the **smaller** of line 13 or line 20. If this is the only Form 1116 you are filing, skip lines 22 through 26 and enter this amount on line 27. Otherwise, complete the appropriate line in Part IV (see instructions) . . . . ▶		21

Part IV Summary of Credits From Separate Parts III (see instructions)

22	Credit for taxes on passive category income	22	
23	Credit for taxes on general category income	23	
24	Credit for taxes on certain income re-sourced by treaty	24	
25	Credit for taxes on lump-sum distributions	25	
26	Add lines 22 through 25		26
27	Enter the **smaller** of line 19 or line 26		27
28	Reduction of credit for international boycott operations. See instructions for line 12		28
29	Subtract line 28 from line 27. This is your **foreign tax credit**. Enter here and on Form 1040, line 47; Form 1040NR, line 45; Form 1041, Schedule G, line 2a; or Form 990-T, line 40a . . . . . . ▶		29

Form **1116** (2010)

Generally, how the foreign tax credit works is that you first compute the tax on the gain in both countries without regard for the credit then subtract the US tax paid from the Canadian tax owing, to arrive at the net tax owed. For instance, using the example in section **3.**, the US tax is $3,000 and the Canadian tax would be between 19.5 percent and 24.13 percent depending on the province you are living in; for this purpose, let's use 20 percent. The tax in Canada would be $4,000 (i.e., $20,000 x 20 percent) before the credit. After applying the credit, you would have $1,000 owing to Canada. In total you still paid the same $4,000 tax you would have paid, you simply split the tax between the two countries.

Note that if you did not use Form 8288-B to reduce your withholding and you paid $10,000 in 2011, you would not be allowed to take a $10,000 credit because $10,000 is not your ultimate tax liability to the US. You would still only be allowed the $3,000 credit. If you did take the $3,000 credit and later found out that your US tax actually turned out to be $2,900 after closing expenses, you would have to go back and file a corrected T1.

See Table 2 for tax filing requirements.

4. State Income Taxes

Just as in Canada, each state has the ability to tax income earned in its state. However, nine states choose not to have an income tax, and those states are: Alaska, Florida, Nevada, New Hampshire, South Dakota, Tennessee, Texas, Washington, and Wyoming. Arizona has a state income tax that ranges from 2.59 to 4.54 percent, where the highest rate starts at $150,000 of income per person ($300,000 per couple). California has an income tax that ranges from 1.25 to 9.55 percent, where the highest rate starts at $47,900 per person.

If you would like to know more about the state individual income taxes, go to the Federation of Tax Administrators website. This link takes you to the 2010 state individual income taxes: www.taxadmin.org/fta/rate/ind_inc.pdf.

Table 2
TAX FILING REQUIREMENTS

Situation	How It's Owned	US Filing Requirements	Potential US Forms to File
Second home — no rental activity	Individual or joint names	None until sold	8288-B, W7, and 1040NR
Second home — with some rental activity	Individual or joint names	Initially	W7 and W-8ECI
		Annually	1040NR, BE-15, and BE-605*
		Upon sale	8288-B and 1040NR
Rental property	Individual or joint names	Initially	W7 and W-8ECI
		Annually	1040NR, BE-15, or BE-605
		Upon sale	8288-B and 1040NR
Rental property	Limited Liability Partnership	Initially	SS-4* and W7
		Quarterly or Annually	1065, 1040NR, 8804, 8805, 8813, BE-15, or BE-605
		Upon sale	8288-B, 1065, and 1040NR
Buy and flip	Individual or joint names	Initially	None
		Upon sale	W7 and 8288-B
		Quarterly or Annually	1040NR, BE-15, or BE-605
Buy and flip	Limited Liability Partnership	Initially	SS-4 and W7
		Upon sale	8288-B
		Quarterly or Annually	1065, 1040NR, 8804, 8805, 8813, BE-15, or BE-605

Note: Application for Employer Identification Number (Form SS-4) is used when an ID number is needed for an entity. The Quarterly Survey of Foreign Direct Investment in the United States (Form BE-605) is the quarterly survey to report positions and transactions between a US company that is affiliated with a foreign parent company. Here are the reporting requirements as of January 2010: www.bea.gov/surveys/pdf/2010current_Reporting_Requirements.pdf.

5. Sales Taxes

The US does not have a national sales tax; sales taxes are imposed by state, county, and city tax authorities. The tax rules vary widely from location to location. Even within a metropolitan area such as Phoenix, tax rates and rules vary among the different cities. Some cities exempt the first or second rental properties, while others require tax starting with the very first rental property. I cannot begin to discuss all of the possibilities; this is an area in which you need to get professional advice. If you are using a property manager, be sure he or she knows all of the applicable rules.

You can find out more about sales tax by going to www.zip2tax.com and using the site's calculator.

4

NONRESIDENT US ESTATE TAX AND PROBATE

Nonresident US Estate Tax and Probate

Unlike Canada, which taxes any previously untaxed income at death, the US system taxes the value of your assets at death. As you might imagine, Canadians have a lot of misinformation about the US estate tax. There is the story about a 45 percent tax levied on a person's net worth. If the estate tax system actually worked like that, there would be reason for surprise, but fortunately important bits of information are missing from this explanation.

In 2009, the US estate tax system provided American citizens and American residents with an exemption of $3.5 million in assets per person. In 2009 only about 1 in 460 deaths resulted in a taxable estate; 99.8 percent of deaths triggered no estate tax.*

As far as I can tell, there is no data on the number of Canadian residents with assets in the US that pay the US nonresident estate tax. I imagine the number is very small, or at least it should be.

---

*Source: Tax Policy Center Table T09-0400.

We occasionally find a case in which a Canadian has passed away and his or her estate has paid US estate tax unnecessarily because his or her advisors did not know that the US-Canada Tax Convention (Treaty) provided complete relief in most situations.

1. Green Card Holders

The taxation of green card holders would normally be outside the scope of this book, but because of its importance as well as the amount of confusion surrounding the tax status of green card holders, I will address the issue in some detail.

The most confusing aspect of being a green card holder is that immigration and tax laws are not congruent. For *immigration purposes*, a person's status as a *lawful permanent resident* will generally be abandoned after the person has been out of the US for more than six months without permission. The United States Citizenship and Immigration Service (USCIS) will not rule on a person's status until he or she attempts to return to the US claiming to be a permanent resident.

For *tax purposes*, a person is treated as a lawful permanent resident until there has been a formal determination that his or her status has been abandoned. Support for this claim can be found in the Joint Committee on Taxation's "General Explanation of the Revenue Provisions of the Deficit Reduction Act of 1984," in which it states:

The Act defines "lawful permanent resident" to mean an individual who has the status of having been lawfully accorded the privilege of residing permanently in the United States as an immigrant in accordance with the immigration laws, if such has not been revoked or administratively or judicially determined to have been abandoned. Therefore, an alien who comes to the United States so infrequently that, on scrutiny, he or she is no longer legally entitled to permanent resident status, will be a resident for tax purposes. The purpose for this requirement of revocation or determination is to prevent aliens from attempting to retain an apparent right to enter or remain in the United States while at-tempting to avoid the tax responsibility that accompanies that right.

The way for a green card holder to give notice of termination of residency is by completing Abandonment of Lawful Permanent Resident Status (Form I-407) in the presence of a diplomatic or consular officer, or at a Port of Entry of the US in the presence of an immigration official.

In summary, unless you have formally terminated your Permanent Residence Status by properly filing immigration Form I-407, you continue to be a resident for tax purposes and must file US returns on your worldwide income. You will also be potentially subject to US estate tax on your worldwide assets at death.

The remainder of this chapter will explain how the US estate tax works for nonresidents and how the Treaty can provide relief.

2. As a Nonresident, When Are You Subject to US Estate Tax?

A nonresident of the US is subject to estate tax on only those assets that are situated in the US at the time of his or her death. The term "asset" has a broad meaning and includes all property, real or personal, tangible or intangible. An example of real property would be land and any buildings on that land. Examples of personal property would be all of the things in the building and would include vehicles. A tangible asset is something you can hold such as gold and collectibles, whereas intangible assets are things you cannot hold directly such as corporations and other financial instruments.

The nonresident estate tax does not apply to US citizens and green card holders resident in Canada (or any other foreign country). US citizens and green card holders are subject to US estate tax on their worldwide assets, regardless of where they were living when they died.

Note: Canadian residents that are *neither* US citizens nor US green card holders are subject to tax on only their US assets at the time of their death. Canadian residents that are *either* US citizens or US green card holders are subject to tax on their worldwide assets, wherever located, at the time of their death.

Not all assets situated in the US are included in the estate of a nonresident, because certain assets are exempt from nonresident estate tax. The most common of these assets include the following:

➤ US bank accounts (e.g., checking, savings, certificate of deposit, and bank money market accounts). Money market mutual funds are not bank accounts and are not exempt. Basically, if it is covered by Federal Deposit Insurance Corporation (FDIC), it is exempt.

➤ Life insurance issued by a US insurer.

➤ Certain debt obligations.

➤ American depository receipts (ADR).

➤ US assets that are held in a foreign entity such as a corporation.

Note: Assets may be subject to probate even if exempt from estate tax. Probate is discussed in section **4.**

Any asset that is not exempt must be included in the nonresident estate. Some assets that may not be obvious to you include:

➤ House furnishings

➤ Vehicles that are licensed and kept in the US

➤ Golf club memberships

➤ US pensions, if there is a survivor benefit

Nonrecourse debt is a subtraction from your assets in determining your taxable estate. Nonrecourse debt is a loan that has only the property as collateral. In other words, the lender cannot go after other assets to collect on the loan if you do not or cannot pay. Not all debt can be subtracted in determining your taxable estate, only nonrecourse debt.

The US Internal Revenue Code allows an exemption of $60,000 of taxable assets per person. However, the US-Canada Tax Treaty allows for a greater exemption if you are willing to disclose your worldwide assets. Article XXIX B (Death Taxes) is reproduced below along with my comments in italics.

2.1 The US-Canada Tax Convention (Treaty) Article XXIX B (Taxes Imposed by Reason of Death)

1. Where the property of an individual who is a resident of a Contracting State passes by reason of the individual's death to an organization referred to in paragraph 1 of Article XXI (Exempt Organizations), and that is a resident of the other Contracting State —

   (a) If the individual is a resident of the United States and the organization is a resident of Canada, the tax consequences in the United States arising out of the passing of the property shall apply as if the organization were a resident of the United States; and

   (b) If the individual is a resident of Canada and the organization is a resident of the United States, the tax consequences in Canada arising out of the passing of the property shall apply as if the individual had disposed of the property for proceeds equal to an amount elected on behalf of the individual for this purpose (in a manner specified by the competent authority of Canada), which amount shall be no less than the individual's cost of the property as determined for purposes of Canadian tax and no greater than the fair market value of the property.

This provision allows Canadians who are neither US citizens nor green card holders a deduction for US estate tax purposes if the charitable bequest is made to a US charity. An estate deduction will also be allowed for a bequest to a Canadian charity to the extent the asset donated was subject to US estate tax.

2. In determining the estate tax imposed by the United States, the estate of an individual (other than a citizen of the United States or green card holder) who was a resident of Canada at the time of the individual's death shall be allowed a unified credit equal to the greater of —

   (a) The amount that bears the same ratio to the credit allowed under the law of the United States to the estate of a citizen of the United States as the value of the part of the individual's gross estate that at the time of the individual's death is situated in the United States bears to the value of the individual's entire gross estate wherever situated; and

The unified credit is a tax credit that is allowed on the assets that are exempted from tax. For example, a nonresident is allowed a $60,000 exemption by law not considering the Treaty. The estate tax on $60,000 is $13,000. The basic unified credit is therefore $13,000, which is the same thing as saying that $60,000 of assets are exempt from tax. The exemption in 2009 was $3,500,000 per person. The unified credit for that amount is $1,455,800. This section says that a Canadian resident is allowed an exemption from US estate tax equal to the ratio of your US assets to your worldwide assets.

Even though the exemption is supposed to decline to $1,000,000 in 2011, I use the $3.5 million amount because it is also possible that congress will increase the exemption from the $3.5 million to 4.5 million level in 2011.

Example: If you purchase a home in the US for $200,000 and your worldwide assets are $1,000,000, your ratio is 20 percent. You then apply the 20 percent to the unified credit amount of

*$1,455,200 (2009). This gives you $291,160 of tax you can avoid. See section **2.2** for more information.*

    (b) The unified credit allowed to the estate of a nonresident not a citizen of the United States under the law of the United States.

        The amount of any unified credit otherwise allowable under this paragraph shall be reduced by the amount of any credit previously allowed with respect to any gift made by the individual. A credit otherwise allowable under subparagraph (a) shall be allowed only if all information necessary for the verification and computation of the credit is provided.

There are two caveats to paragraph (a). The first one is that you must reduce the credit (exemption) by the amount of credit (exemption) previously taken under the US gift tax rules. The second caveat is that you must file the US Gift Tax Return (Form 709-NA) and provide proof of the computation. Primarily the IRS are after proof of the denominator (worldwide assets).

Caution: *When calculating the credit, use the percentage of the credit allowed for Americans, not the tax owing on the assets resulting in applying the percentage to the asset equivalent.*

The second caveat is that you must report all of your worldwide assets so that value can be demonstrated. It makes sense that the IRS would want this; given that it is giving you a higher exemption based on world-wide assets, the IRS would want to make sure the number is accurate.

3. In determining the estate tax imposed by the United States on an individual's estate with respect to property that passes to the surviving spouse of the individual (within the meaning of the law of the United States) and that would qualify for the estate tax marital deduction under the law of the United States if the surviving spouse were a citizen of the United States and all applicable elections were properly made (in this paragraph

and paragraph 4 referred to as "qualifying property"), a nonrefundable credit computed in accordance with the provisions of paragraph 4 shall be allowed in addition to the unified credit allowed to the estate under paragraph 2 or under the law of the United States, provided that —

(a) The individual was at the time of death a citizen of the United States or a resident of either Contracting State;

(b) The surviving spouse was at the time of the individual's death a resident of either Contracting State;

(c) If both the individual and the surviving spouse were residents of the United States at the time of the individual's death, one or both was a citizen of Canada; and

(d) The executor of the decedent's estate elects the benefits of this paragraph and waives irrevocably the benefits of any estate tax marital deduction that would be allowed under the law of the United States on a United States Federal estate tax return filed for the individual's estate by the date on which a qualified domestic trust election could be made under the law of the United States.

US citizens are allowed to pass assets to their spouse at death without estate tax. Except for the benefits of the Treaty, noncitizen spouses are not allowed to receive unlimited amounts of assets to be passed to them by their deceased spouse. This provision eases the impact of that law through a marital credit. The credit is calculated in paragraph 4.

4. The amount of the credit allowed under paragraph 3 shall equal the lesser of —

(a) The unified credit allowed under paragraph 2 or under the law of the United States (determined without regard to any credit allowed previously with respect to any gift made by the individual), and

(b) The amount of estate tax that would otherwise be imposed by the United States on the transfer of qualifying property.

The amount of estate tax that would otherwise be imposed by the United States on the transfer of qualifying property shall equal the amount by which the estate tax (before allowable credits) that would be imposed by the United States if the qualifying property were included in computing the taxable estate exceeds the estate tax (before allowable credits) that would be so imposed if the qualifying property were not so included. Solely for purposes of determining other credits allowed under the law of the United States, the credit provided under paragraph 3 shall be allowed after such other credits.

5. Where an individual was a resident of the United States immediately before the individual's death, for the purposes of subsections 70(5.2) and (6) of the *Income Tax Act*, both the individual and the individual's spouse shall be deemed to have been resident in Canada immediately before the individual's death. Where a trust that would be a trust described in subsection 70(6) of that Act, if its trustees that were residents or citizens of the United States or domestic corporations under the law of the United States were residents of Canada, requests the competent authority of Canada to do so, the competent authority may agree, subject to terms and conditions satisfactory to such competent authority, to treat the trust for the purposes of that Act as being resident in Canada for such time as may be stipulated in the agreement.

This paragraph is generally not applicable to residents of Canada.

6. In determining the amount of Canadian tax payable by an individual who immediately before death was a resident of Canada, or by a trust described in subsection

70(6) of the *Income Tax Act* (or a trust which is treated as being resident in Canada under the provisions of paragraph 5), the amount of any Federal or state estate or inheritance taxes payable in the United States (not exceeding, where the individual was a citizen of the United States or a former citizen referred to in paragraph 2 of Article XXIX (Miscellaneous Rules), the amount of estate and inheritance taxes that would have been payable if the individual were not a citizen or former citizen of the United States) in respect of property situated within the United States shall —

(a) To the extent that such estate or inheritance taxes are imposed upon the individual's death, be allowed as a deduction from the amount of any Canadian tax otherwise payable by the individual for the taxation year in which the individual died on the total of —

   (i) Any income, profits, or gains of the individual arising [within the meaning of paragraph 3 of Article XXIV (Elimination of Double Taxation)] in the United States in that year; and

   (ii) Where the value, at the individual's death, of the individual's entire gross estate wherever situated (determined under the law of the United States) exceeded 1.2 million US dollars or its equivalent in Canadian dollars, any income, profits, or gains of the individual for that year from property situated in the United States at that time; and

(b) To the extent that such estate or inheritance taxes are imposed upon the death of the individual's surviving spouse, be allowed as a deduction from the amount of any Canadian tax otherwise payable by the trust for its taxation year in which that spouse dies on any income, profits, or gains of the trust for that year arising [within the meaning of paragraph 3 of Article XXIV (Elimination of Double Taxation)] in the United States or from property situated in the United States at the time of death of the spouse.

For purposes of this paragraph, property shall be treated as situated within the United States if it is so treated for estate tax purposes under the law of the United States as in effect on *March 17, 1995*, subject to any subsequent changes thereof that the competent authorities of the Contracting States have agreed to apply for the purposes of this paragraph. The deduction allowed under this paragraph shall take into account the deduction for any income tax paid or accrued to the United States that is provided under paragraph 2(a), 4(a) or 5(b) of Article XXIV (Elimination of Double Taxation).

This paragraph sets out the calculation of Canadian income taxes payable by a resident of Canada due to death. It also allows for a credit of US estate tax paid.

7. In determining the amount of estate tax imposed by the United States on the estate of an individual who was a resident or citizen of the United States at the time of death, or upon the death of a surviving spouse with respect to a qualified domestic trust created by such an individual or the individual's executor or surviving spouse, a credit shall be allowed against such tax imposed in respect of property situated outside the United States, for the federal and provincial income taxes payable in Canada in respect of such property by reason of the death of the individual or, in the case of a qualified domestic trust, the individual's surviving spouse. Such credit shall be computed in accordance with the following rules:

(a) A credit otherwise allowable under this paragraph shall be allowed regardless of whether the identity of the taxpayer under the law of Canada corresponds to that under the law of the United States.

(b) The amount of a credit allowed under this paragraph shall be computed in accordance with the provisions and subject to the limitations of the law of the United States regarding credit for foreign death taxes (as it may be amended from time to time without changing the general principle hereof), as though the income tax imposed by Canada were a creditable tax under that law.

(c) A credit may be claimed under this paragraph for an amount of federal or provincial income tax payable in Canada only to the extent that no credit or deduction is claimed for such amount in determining any other tax imposed by the United States, other than the estate tax imposed on property in a qualified domestic trust upon the death of the surviving spouse.

This paragraph allows for a credit of Canadian federal and provincial taxes paid, on the US estate tax return.

8. Provided that the value, at the time of death, of the entire gross estate wherever situated of an individual who was a resident of Canada (other than a citizen of the United States) at the time of death does not exceed 1.2 million US dollars or its equivalent in Canadian dollars, the United States may impose its estate tax upon property forming part of the estate of the individual only if any gain derived by the individual from the alienation of such property would have been subject to income taxation by the United States in accordance with Article XIII (Gains).

This paragraph is an exemption of US estate tax for residents of Canada with estates of $1.2 million USD or less.

2.2 How the US nonresident estate tax works

As a Canadian you are allowed an exemption equal to the pro-rata amount an American is allowed. The ratio is based on your US assets over your worldwide assets. That ratio is then applied to the exemption to arrive at an exemption amount.

Example 1: Margret purchased a home in the US one year ago at a price of $120,000. She furnished the house for $40,000. Margret died when the property had a fair market value of $125,000.

Margret's US estate when she died was valued at $150,000 ($125,000 for the house and $25,000 for furnishing). Note that the value of the furnishing declined from $40,000 to $25,000 based on fair market value at the date of death. Margret's worldwide estate was valued at $5,000,000. This results in 3 percent of her assets being located in the US and this percentage is applied to credit of $1,455,800 (tax on $3,500,000), resulting in an available credit of $43,674. There was $2,500 of US administrative expenses associated with the death. (See Sample 12.)

Note: Even though the credit available is $43,674, the tax before the credit is only $38,778 and credit is therefore limited to the amount of the tax otherwise owing. This type of credit cannot generate a refund; it is limited to lesser of the credit amount or the gross estate tax.

Caution: When calculating the credit, use the percentage of the exemption allowed to Americans. Do not apply the percentage to your US assets, and then calculate the estate tax on that number. Advisors occasionally take shortcuts when describing to clients how the Treaty works.

The result of using the ratio of the credit allowed Americans ($1,455,800 x 3% = $43,674) is that you receive a benefit greater than if you were simply to apply the credit based on tax that would be owed on the asset amount you would arrive at by applying the ratio times the amount of assets that can be excluded ($3,500,000 x 3% = $105,000). Clearly, if you were to calculate the tax using this method, there would be tax due since $105,000 is less than the US assets of $150,000.

UNITED STATES ESTATE TAX RETURN (FORM 706-NA)

Form **706-NA** (Rev. September 2009) Department of the Treasury Internal Revenue Service	**United States Estate (and Generation-Skipping Transfer) Tax Return** **Estate of nonresident not a citizen of the United States** To be filed for decedents dying after December 31, 2008. ▶ See separate instructions.	OMB No. 1545-0531

Attach supplemental documents and translations. Show amounts in U.S. dollars.

Part I Decedent, Executor, and Attorney

1a Decedent's first (given) name and middle initial	b Decedent's last (family) name	2 U.S. taxpayer ID number (if any)
Margret		

3 Place of death	4 Domicile at time of death	5 Citizenship (nationality)	6 Date of death
		Canada	

7a Date of birth	b Place of birth	8 Business or occupation

	9a Name of executor	10a Name of attorney for estate
In United States	b Address	b Address
	11a Name of executor	12a Name of attorney for estate
Outside United States	b Address	b Address

Part II Tax Computation

1	Taxable estate from Schedule B, line 9	1	149,925
2	Total taxable gifts of tangible or intangible property located in the U.S., transferred (directly or indirectly) by the decedent after December 31, 1976, and not included in the gross estate (see section 2511)	2	0
3	Total. Add lines 1 and 2.	3	149,925
4	Tentative tax on the amount on line 3 (see instructions)	4	38,778
5	Tentative tax on the amount on line 2 (see instructions)	5	0
6	Gross estate tax. Subtract line 5 from line 4	6	38,778
7	Unified credit. Enter smaller of line 6 amount or maximum allowed (see instructions)	7	38,778
8	Balance. Subtract line 7 from line 6	8	0
9	Other credits (see instructions) 9		
10	Credit for tax on prior transfers. Attach Schedule Q, Form 706 10		
11	Total. Add lines 9 and 10	11	0
12	Net estate tax. Subtract line 11 from line 8	12	0
13	Total generation-skipping transfer tax. Attach Schedule R, Form 706	13	0
14	**Total transfer taxes.** Add lines 12 and 13	14	0
15	Earlier payments. See instructions and attach explanation	15	0
16	Balance due. Subtract line 15 from line 14 (see instructions)	16	0

Under penalties of perjury, I declare that I have examined this return, including accompanying schedules and statements, and to the best of my knowledge and belief, it is true, correct, and complete. I understand that a complete return requires listing all property constituting the part of the decedent's gross estate (as defined by the statute) situated in the United States. Declaration of preparer (other than executor) is based on all information of which preparer has any knowledge.

Sign Here	▶ Signature of executor	▶ Date
	▶ Signature of executor	▶ Date

Paid Preparer's Use Only	Preparer's signature ▶	Date	Check if self-employed ☐	Preparer's SSN or PTIN
	Firm's name (or yours, if self-employed), address, and ZIP code ▶		EIN Phone no. ( )	

For Privacy Act and Paperwork Reduction Act Notice, see the separate instructions.   Cat. No. 10145K   Form **706-NA** (Rev. 9-2009)

Sample 12 — Continued

Part III   General Information

		Yes	No			Yes	No
1a	Did the decedent die testate?		✔	**7**	Did the decedent make any transfer (of property that was located in the United States at either the time of the transfer or the time of death) described in sections 2035, 2036, 2037, or 2038 (see the instructions for Form 706, Schedule G)?		
b	Were letters testamentary or of administration granted for the estate?						✔
	If granted to persons other than those filing the return, include names and addresses on page 1.				*If "Yes," attach Schedule G, Form 706.*		
2	Did the decedent, at the time of death, own any:			**8**	At the date of death, were there any trusts in existence that were created by the decedent and that included property located in the United States either when the trust was created or when the decedent died?		
a	Real property located in the United States?	✔					
b	U.S. corporate stock?		✔				✔
c	Debt obligations of (1) a U.S. person, or (2) the United States, a state or any political subdivision, or the District of Columbia?		✔		*If "Yes," attach Schedule G, Form 706.*		
d	Other property located in the United States?	✔		**9**	At the date of death, did the decedent:		
3	Was the decedent engaged in business in the United States at the date of death?		✔	**a**	Have a general power of appointment over any property located in the United States?		✔
4	At the date of death, did the decedent have access, personally or through an agent, to a safe deposit box located in the United States?		✔	**b**	Or, at any time, exercise or release the power? *If "Yes" to either a or b, attach Schedule H, Form 706.*		✔
5	At the date of death, did the decedent own any property located in the United States as a joint tenant with right of survivorship; as a tenant by the entirety; or, with surviving spouse, as community property?		✔	**10a**	Have federal gift tax returns ever been filed?		✔
	If "Yes," attach Schedule E, Form 706.			**b**	Periods covered ▶		
				c	IRS offices where filed ▶		
6a	Had the decedent ever been a citizen or resident of the United States (see instructions)?		✔	**11**	Does the gross estate in the United States include any interests in property transferred to a "skip person" as defined in the instructions to Schedule R of Form 706?		✔
b	If "Yes," did the decedent lose U.S. citizenship or residency within 10 years of death? (see instructions).				*If "Yes," attach Schedules R and/or R-1, Form 706.*		

Schedule A. Gross Estate in the United States (see instructions)

	Yes	No
Do you elect to value the decedent's gross estate at a date or dates after the decedent's death (as authorized by section 2032)? ▶		✔

To make the election, you must check this box "Yes." If you check "Yes," complete **all** columns. If you check "No," complete columns (a), (b), and (e); you may leave columns (c) and (d) blank or you may use them to expand your column (b) description.

(a) Item no.	(b) Description of property and securities For securities, give CUSIP number	(c) Alternate valuation date	(d) Alternate value in U.S. dollars	(e) Value at date of death in U.S. dollars
1	Single family home at 123 State Street, Anywhere USA	N/A	N/A	125,000
2	Furnishings at 123 State Street, Anywhere USA	N/A	N/A	25,000
	(If you need more space, attach additional sheets of same size.)			
Total .			N/A	150,000

Schedule B. Taxable Estate

Caution. You must document lines 2 and 4 for the deduction on line 5 to be allowed.

1	Gross estate in the United States (Schedule A total)	**1**	150,000
2	Gross estate outside the United States (see instructions)	**2**	4,850,000
3	Entire gross estate wherever located. Add amounts on lines 1 and 2	**3**	5,000,000
4	Amount of funeral expenses, administration expenses, decedent's debts, mortgages and liens, and losses during administration. Attach itemized schedule. (see instructions).	**4**	2,500
5	Deduction for expenses, claims, etc. Divide line 1 by line 3 and multiply the result by line 4	**5**	75
6	Charitable deduction (attach Schedule O, Form 706) and marital deduction (attach Schedule M, Form 706, and computation)	**6**	0
7	State death tax deduction (see instructions)	**7**	0
8	Total deductions. Add lines 5, 6, and 7	**8**	75
9	Taxable estate. Subtract line 8 from line 1. Enter here and on line 1 of Part II	**9**	149,925

Form **706-NA** (Rev. 9-2009)

Caution: Just because there will be no estate tax due does not mean that you do not have to file an estate tax return. You must file Form 706-NA to prove the denominator (i.e., your worldwide assets).

Example 2: Let's say that you are married and your worldwide assets total $10,000,000, and you have 50 percent or $5,000,000 of those assets in an office building in Fort Lauderdale, Florida. Your exemption would be $727,900 ($1,455,800 x 50%). If you leave the building to your spouse, you would be entitled to a marital credit that would be another $727,900. The tax on $5,000,000 is $2,130,800 (from tax table) before the exemption. After subtracting $1,455,800 (your exemption of $727,900, doubled to $1,455,800 due to marital credit) from your gross estate tax, you have $675,000 of US estate tax on $5,000,000 of assets, for an effective tax rate of 13.5 percent. Of course, this is with no planning at all; with some planning the US estate tax can be reduced substantially or even eliminated.

The Canadian marital credit is described in the Treaty and on the last page of the instructions to Form 706-NA at www.irs.gov/pub/irs-pdf/i706na.pdf. The estate tax rate schedule is on page 4, Table A of the Instructions.

3. A Dollar Is Not Always a Dollar

You would think that reporting the fair market value of real estate would be a straightforward process, but it can be very complicated. You may also be surprised to know that the way you hold title to a property can influence the fair market value. This section begins by defining terms which are different between the two countries. I finish by explaining how holding the property in an entity such as a partnership or corporation may reduce the value for estate planning purposes and therefore potentially reduce any US estate tax payable.

When reporting the value of your US assets, you must use the fair market value (FMV). The definitions of FMV are different in the US and Canada.

In United States tax law, the definition of *fair market value* is found in the United States Supreme Court decision in the Cartwright case:

The fair market value is the price at which the property would change hands between a willing buyer and a willing seller, neither being under any compulsion to buy or to sell and both having reasonable knowledge of relevant facts.

The term *fair market value* is used throughout the Internal Revenue Code and among other federal statutory laws in the US including bankruptcy, many state laws, and several regulatory bodies.

In Canada, the term *fair market value* is not explicitly defined in the *Income Tax Act*. That said, Mr. Justice Cattanach in *Henderson Estate, Bank of New Year v. M.N.R.*, (1973) C.T.C. 636 at p. 644 articulates the concept as follows:

The statute does not define the expression "fair market value," but the expression has been defined in many different ways depending generally on the subject matter which the person seeking to define it had in mind. I do not think it necessary to attempt an exact definition of the expression as used in the statute other than to say that the words must be construed in accordance with the common understanding of them. That common understanding I take to mean the highest price an asset might reasonably be expected to bring if sold by the owner in the normal method applicable to the asset in question in the ordinary course of business in a market not exposed to any undue stresses and composed of willing buyers and sellers dealing at arm's length and under no compulsion to buy or sell. I would add that the foregoing understanding as I have expressed it in a general way includes what I conceive to be the essential element which is an open and unrestricted market in which the price is hammered out between willing and informed buyers and sellers on the anvil of supply and demand. These definitions are equally applicable to "fair market value" and "market value" and it is doubtful if the word "fair" adds anything to the words "market value."

Canada Revenue Agency (CRA) lists the following definition in its online dictionary:

Fair market value generally means the highest price, expressed in dollars, that a property would bring in an open and unrestricted market between a willing buyer and a willing seller who are both knowledgeable, informed, and prudent, and who are acting independently of each other.

As you can see, the US and Canadian concepts of fair market value are very similar, but not exactly the same. When dealing with the IRS or when filing US returns, it is important that you use the US meaning of Fair Market Value.

That being said, there are a number of factors that influence what a willing buyer is willing to pay. A couple of the more common factors are a lack of control and a lack of marketability (liquidity). If one or both of these factors exist, a discount is applied before arriving at FMV.

The discount for lack of control is pretty straightforward. Would you pay the same amount for an asset over which you had no or very little say as you would for an asset which you can control? Here is an example: Most people would readily exchange one dollar for another dollar (i.e., provide me change for my one dollar bill) if there were no restriction on what they could do with that dollar. It would elicit an entirely different response if I asked for change for my dollar bill, but told you that you could not spend that dollar without my permission.

The liquidity discount or liquid asset has some or more of the following features according to Wikipedia:

It can be sold rapidly, with minimal loss of value, any time within market hours. The essential characteristic of a liquid market is that there are ready and willing buyers and sellers at all times. Another elegant definition of liquidity is the probability that the next trade is executed at a price equal to the last one. A market may be considered deeply liquid if there are ready and willing buyers and sellers in large quantities. This is related to the concept of market depth that can be measured as the units that can be sold or bought for a given price impact. The opposite concept is that of market breadth measured as the price impact per unit of liquidity.

An illiquid asset is an asset which is not readily salable due to uncertainty about its value or the lack of a market in which it is regularly traded. The mortgage related assets which resulted in the subprime mortgage crisis are examples of illiquid assets, as their value is not readily determinable despite being secured by real property. Another example is an asset such as a large block of stock, the sale of which affects the market value.

When holding your real estate in a business entity in which the other business owners cannot readily sell their shares or membership interests and do not own a greater than 50 percent interest in the business, you will most likely receive a discount for both of these factors (lack of marketability and minority discounts). The discounts applied vary based on the facts and circumstances of the business, but a common combined discount is 30 percent. Therefore, if you have real estate valued in the partnership at $100,000 and assuming no other assets in the partnership, the value of the partnership might be around $70,000 if these discounts are applied. The $70,000 is the number you would report as the value of your US assets on an estate tax return. An appraisal from a qualified appraiser is required to prove the discount.

Tip: Holding assets in a business entity may reduce your US estate tax liability.

4. Probate

Probate is the legal process of administering the estate of a deceased person by resolving all claims and distributing the deceased person's property under a valid will.

Probate generally lasts several months, and it can take over a year before all of the property is distributed. Costs can range from minimal to expensive, depending on the state and the complexity of the probate. One complexity that may come up with some regularity is having a Quebec will. Not only might the will be in French and therefore require official translation, it is based on Napoleonic law versus common law.

Avoiding probate can be accomplished by having the property pass directly to heirs contractually, such as through a beneficiary designation like those of insurance policies or retirement plans. Property can also pass contractually when it is owned jointly with rights of survivorship. There are things that can be done with bank and brokerage accounts that are very much like naming a beneficiary and it is called owning the property as "payable on death." Just like a beneficiary designation, you can name and/or change beneficiaries at any time prior to death. If married, changes can be made prior to the survivor's death. This concept is very similar to beneficiary deeds described in Chapter 2.

Note: If you have a bank account in the US that is not held in an entity such as a corporation or partnership, you should consider setting up Paid on Death (POD) accounts to avoid probate. You can do something similar, called Transfer on Death (TOD) for brokerage accounts.

Another way to avoid probate is to establish a revocable living trust. Any assets held in the trust pass to the beneficiaries by the terms of the trust. Another advantage of revocable living trusts is that they are private. Since the trust is not filed with the court and there is no need for probate, all the terms of the trust are kept private. However, a will is a public document that can be viewed by anyone after the person has died and the probate has been settled.

As I mentioned in Chapter 2, a revocable living trust may not be necessary if the property is in a state that allows beneficiary deeds. It would also not be needed if the property is held in some sort of foreign entity such as a corporation or partnership. Lastly, the revocable living trust would not be needed for small properties in which the cost of probate would be less than the cost of the trust.

Caution: Be very careful about adding children to the title as joint owners to avoid probate. While this strategy will certainly avoid probate, it creates a whole host of other, potentially worse problems. The first such problem would be potential gift tax consequences. If you add a child as a joint owner, you may have just gifted half the value of the property to the child. In addition, you now subject the property to the claims of the children, such as divorce, bankruptcy, lawsuits, etc.

4.1 State-specific rules of probate

Arizona and Florida do not regulate probate fees, but they must be "reasonable." Arizona requires a four-month period in which to present a claim against the estate, therefore no Arizona probate can be completed in less than four months. In Florida, the minimum time is three months.

California sets the maximum fees that attorneys can charge for probate. The fees are —

- 4 percent of the first $100,000 of the estate;

- 3 percent of the next $100,000;

- 2 percent of the next $800,000;

- 1 percent for the next $9,000,000; and

- 0.5 percent of the next $15,000,000.

The court will determine the fee for amounts greater than $25,000,000.

If the executor receives a fee, he or she will be paid according to the same fee schedule, effectively doubling the fees. If there are complications, the attorney and executor can ask the judge to approve higher fees. There are also various court fees that typically run about $1,000 to $3,000. Probate in California will take, at a minimum, about nine months to be completed.

5

OTHER INFORMATION YOU SHOULD KNOW

Other Information You Should Know

As with any significant undertaking, there are many things to consider when buying property in a foreign country. In this chapter I will discuss important things you should know that I have not discussed in the previous chapters.

1. Department of Commerce Filing Requirements

A series of forms that are frequently overlooked are those from the Bureau of Economic Analysis (BEA), a division of the US Department of Commerce. These forms are typically not completed by advisors because of their obscurity, and because they are not tax forms accountants generally do not consider it their responsibility.

The BEA produces comprehensive statistics on foreign direct investment in the US. The statistics, which are the world's most comprehensive and accurate, are obtained from mandatory surveys. Even if you are exempt from filing, you are still required to file Claim for Exemption (Form BE-15), to prove your exemption. In other words, even if you would have been exempt except for the fact you failed to file the Claim for Exemption, you are liable for all of the penalties and possible imprisonment for a company that is not exempt. (See Sample 13.)

To be eligible for exemption, your assets, sales, or net income have to be $40 million or less. This makes virtually everyone reading this book exempt *if* they file Form BE-15. See Table 3 for a flowchart of the proper BE-15 form to file.

Note: If you are buying the property for personal use (i.e., not for a business reason), you are exempt and do not have to file Form BE-15. You do not have to file the form every time you buy a property. After you have filed to claim exemption on your first property, you are free from future filing until you exceed the $40 million threshold.

If you convert the property from personal to business use, you will need to file the form.

Caution: A "foreign person" is defined as anyone that is a resident outside the US and is subject to the jurisdiction of another country. That means that if you are a US citizen living in Canada, investing in US real estate, you are required to complete these forms.

Obviously, with a $40 million threshold, a very large portion of investors in US real estate will qualify for the exemption. However, the form must be filed for the claim for exemption. Consider going to a different advisor if your advisor is not aware of the BEA forms or is unwilling to prepare them for you.

2. Overview of the Buying Process

There are many differences between buying real estate in Canada and buying real estate in the US. The biggest difference may be title insurance, but there are also differences in the closing process and the length of time to qualify for a US mortgage. Your realtor will guide you through the process, but you should know the basic differences before you start.

Sample 13
CLAIM FOR EXEMPTION (FORM BE-15)

FORM **BE-15 Claim for Exemption** (REV. 10/2009)
FORM CODE X

OMB No. 0608-0034: Approval Expires 02/29/2012 | **BEA Identification Number** ⟶

BEA
BUREAU OF ECONOMIC ANALYSIS
U.S. DEPARTMENT OF COMMERCE

MANDATORY — CONFIDENTIAL
2009 ANNUAL SURVEY OF FOREIGN DIRECT INVESTMENT IN THE UNITED STATES
CLAIM FOR EXEMPTION FROM FILING FORM BE-15A, BE-15B, OR BE-15(EZ)

DUE DATE: MAY 31, 2010

MAIL REPORTS TO:
U.S. Department of Commerce
Bureau of Economic Analysis, BE-49(A)
Washington, DC 20230
OR

DELIVER REPORTS TO:
U.S. Department of Commerce
Bureau of Economic Analysis, BE-49(A)
Shipping and Receiving Section, M100
1441 L Street, NW
Washington, DC 20005
OR

ELECTRONIC FILING: www.bea.gov/efile
OR

FAX REPORTS TO: (202) 606-1905*

*See the **NOTE** at the bottom of this page if you plan to fax your report to BEA.

ASSISTANCE:
Email: be12/15@bea.gov
Telephone: (202) 606-5577
Copies of blank forms: www.bea.gov/fdi
Definitions of key terms: See page 4.

A. Name and address of U.S. business enterprise – If a label has been affixed, make any changes directly on the label. If a label has not been affixed, enter the BEA Identification Number of this U.S. affiliate, if available, in the box at the upper right hand corner of this page.

1002 Name of U.S. affiliate
0

1010 c/o (care of)
0

1003 Street or P.O. Box
0

1004 City | 0998 State
0 | 0

1005 ZIP Code | OR | Foreign Postal Code
0 | | 0

B. Enter Employer Identification Number(s) used by the U.S. business enterprise to file income and payroll taxes.

Primary | Other
1006 1 _ _ | 2 _ _

RESPONSE REQUIRED

Section 806.4 of 15 CFR, Chapter VIII, requires that all persons subject to the reporting requirements of the BE-15 Survey respond, whether or not they are contacted by BEA. It also requires that persons who are contacted by BEA about reporting in this survey, must respond in writing. They may respond by:

- filing the properly completed Form BE-15A, BE-15B, or BE-15(EZ) by May 31, 2010, as required;
- completing and returning the Form BE-15 Claim for Exemption From Filing Form BE-15A, BE-15B, or BE-15(EZ), by May 31, 2010;
- certifying in writing, by May 31, 2010 to the fact that the person had no direct investment within the purview of the reporting requirements of the BE-15 survey.

WHICH SECTIONS TO COMPLETE?

Complete items A and B above, and the Person to Consult Concerning Questions About This Report and the Certification at the bottom of this page. Also, please review the questions below to determine the additional information required.

I Were at least 10 percent of the voting rights in your business directly or indirectly owned by a foreign person or entity at the end of your fiscal year that ended in calendar year 2009?

☐ Yes – Continue with question II below. **Your business is hereinafter referred to as a "U.S. affiliate."**

☐ No – Complete item 2(a) or (b) or (c) or (e) on page 3. If your business has been liquidated or dissolved, complete (a) or (b). Do not complete questions II, III or IV below.

II Were more than 50 percent of the voting rights in this U.S. affiliate owned by another U.S. affiliate, or was this U.S. affiliate merged into another U.S. affiliate at the end of this U.S. affiliate's fiscal year that ended in calendar year 2009?

☐ Yes – Yes continue with question III below.
☐ No – Skip to question IV below.

III Will the data for this U.S. affiliate be consolidated into the 2009 BE-15 report filed for the U.S. affiliate that owns it more than 50 percent, or be included on the 2009 BE-15 report filed for the U.S. affiliate into which it was merged?

☐ Yes – Complete item 2d(1) or 2d(2) on page 3.
☐ No – Contact BEA for guidance.

IV Did **any one** of the items – Total assets, Sales or gross operating revenues, or Net income (loss) – for the U.S. affiliate (not just the foreign parent's share) exceed $40 million at the end of, or for, its fiscal year that ended in calendar year 2009?

☐ Yes – You are not eligible to file Form BE-15 Claim for Exemption and must file either a Form BE-15A, BE-15B, or BE-15(EZ). Copies of blank forms can be found at: **www.bea.gov/fdi**

☐ No – Complete items 1a through 1h on page 2. Do NOT complete page 3.

MANDATORY CONFIDENTIALITY PENALTIES ➔ This survey is being conducted under the International Investment and Trade in Services Survey Act (P.L. 94-472, 90 Stat. 2059, 22 U.S.C. 3101-3108, as amended). The filing of reports is mandatory and the Act provides that your report to this Bureau is confidential. Whoever fails to report may be subject to penalties. See page 4 for more details.

PERSON TO CONSULT CONCERNING QUESTIONS ABOUT THIS REPORT — Enter name and address

1000 Name
0

1029 Address
0

1030 0

1031 0

1001 Telephone number | Area code | Number | Extension

0999 FAX number | Area code | Number

CERTIFICATION — The undersigned official certifies that this report has been prepared in accordance with the applicable instructions, is complete, and is substantially accurate except that estimates may have been provided where data are not available from customary accounting records or precise data could not be obtained without undue burden.

Authorized official's signature | Date

0990 Print or type name | 0991 Print or type title
0 | 0

0992 Telephone number | 0993 FAX number
0 | 0

May FAX and/or email be used in correspondence between your enterprise and BEA, including FAX'ed reports, and/or to discuss questions relating to this survey that may contain confidential information about your company?

NOTE: The internet and telephone systems are not secure means of transmitting confidential information unless it is encrypted. If you choose to communicate with BEA via FAX or electronic mail, BEA cannot guarantee the security of the information during transmission, but will treat information we receive as confidential in accordance with Section 5(c) of the International Investment and Trade in Services Survey Act.

1027 Email: 1 ☐ Yes (If yes, please print your email address.) ⟶ Email address (Please print)
2 ☐ No
0
1028

1032 FAX: 1 ☐ Yes 2 ☐ No

BASIS OF CLAIM FOR EXEMPTION

Select one type of exemption -- either based on Value (#1 below) or based on one of the reasons listed under Other Exemptions (#2 on page 3). Please check box corresponding to the type of exemption you are claiming.

1. **Exemption based on Value** *(check box below)*

   0100 **1** [1]

   If item 1 is applicable, complete ALL items (1.a. through 1.h.) below.

   The U.S. business enterprise was a U.S. affiliate of a foreign person at the end of its fiscal year that ended in calendar year 2009, but is exempt from filing Form BE-15A, BE-15B, or BE-15(EZ) because, on a fully consolidated basis, **none** of the following three items for the U.S. affiliate (not just the foreign parent's share) exceeded $40 million (positive or negative) at the end of, or for, its fiscal year that ended in calendar year 2009:

   - Total assets (do not net out liabilities);
   - Sales or gross operating revenues, excluding sales taxes; and
   - Net income (loss) for FY 2009, after provision for U.S. Federal, state, and local income taxes.

   Rounding – Report currency amounts in U.S. dollars rounded to thousands (omitting 000). **Do not enter amounts in the shaded portions of each line.**
   Example – If amount is $1,334,891.00 report as: →

Bil.	Mil.	Thous.	Dols.
	1	335	000

		Bil.	Mil.	Thous.	Dols.
a. Total assets at the close of the fiscal year that ended in calendar year 2009 – Do not net out liabilities.	2109	$			000
b. Sales or gross operating revenues for the fiscal year that ended in calendar year 2009, excluding sales taxes – Do not give gross margin.	2149				000
c. Net income (loss) for the fiscal year that ended in calendar year 2009, after provision for U.S. Federal, state, and local income taxes.	2159				000
d. Total liabilities at the close of the fiscal year that ended in calendar year 2009.	2114	$			000

   1 [3] **Please check box if total liabilities are zero.**

   e. Major product(s) or service(s) of the fully consolidated domestic U.S. affiliate – Briefly describe the major product(s) and/or service(s) of the U.S. affiliate. If a product, also state what is done to it, i.e., whether it is mined, manufactured, sold at wholesale, transported, packaged, etc. (For example, "manufacture widgets.")

   1163 [0]

   f. Industry code of the fully consolidated domestic U.S. affiliate – Enter the 4-digit International Surveys Industry (ISI) code of the industry with the largest sales or gross operating revenues. For a full explanation of each code, see the *Guide to Industry Classifications for International Surveys, 2007*. A copy of this guide can be found on our web site at: www.bea.gov/naics2007

   ISI Code 1164 [1]

   g. Please enter the country of the foreign parent in the box below. The foreign parent is the FIRST person or entity outside the U.S. in a chain of ownership that has a 10 percent or more **voting** interest in this U.S. affiliate. See diagram below for an illustration of foreign parent.
   Country of foreign parent

   BEA USE ONLY 3016 [1]

   h. Please enter the country of the ultimate beneficial owner (UBO) in the box below. The UBO is that person or entity, proceeding up the ownership chain beginning with and including the foreign parent, that is not more than 50 percent owned or controlled by another person or entity. See diagram below for an illustration of UBO.
   Country of UBO

   BEA USE ONLY 3022 [1]

ILLUSTRATION OF FOREIGN PARENT AND ULTIMATE BENEFICIAL OWNER (UBO)

Foreign Company X **(UBO)**
>50 Percent
Foreign Company Y **(Foreign Parent)**

Foreign
United States

10 to 100 Percent

U.S. affiliate A
U.S. affiliate B

Foreign Company Y is the foreign parent but it is not the UBO because it is more than 50 percent owned or controlled by Foreign Company X. Foreign Company X is the UBO.

Foreign Company Y directly owns 10 percent or more of the voting rights of U.S. affiliate A.

U.S. affiliate B is indirectly owned by Foreign Company Y through U.S. affiliate A.

NOTE: Arrows connecting boxes represent direction of ownership. In the illustration above, if Foreign Company Y does not have at least a 10 percent indirect voting interest in U.S. affiliate B, then U.S. affiliate B is exempt from filing Form BE-15. In addition, if U.S. affiliate A owns more than 50 percent of U.S. affiliate B, then the data for U.S. affiliate B should be consolidated on the BE-15 report filed for U.S. affiliate A.

FORM BE-15 Claim For Exemption (REV. 10/2009)   Page 2

Select one type of exemption either based on one of the reasons listed under Other Exemptions (#2 below) or based on Value (#1 on page 2). Please check box corresponding to the type of exemption you are claiming.

This U.S. business enterprise is exempt from filing a Form BE-15A, BE-15B, or BE-15(EZ) because:

2. Other Exemptions *(check box below)*

(a) 0170 **1** ☐ This U.S. business enterprise was a U.S. affiliate of a foreign person or entity at some time during calendar year 2009 but ceased to be a U.S. affiliate before the end of the fiscal year that ended in calendar year 2009.

Give date foreign ownership ceased or went below 10 percent, or when the business was liquidated or dissolved.

7012	Month	Day	Year
	1		

(b) 0110 **1** ☐ This U.S. business enterprise was not a U.S. affiliate of a foreign person or entity at any time during calendar year 2009 but had been a U.S. affiliate of a foreign person at some time before January 1, 2009.

Give date foreign ownership ceased or went below 10 percent, or when the business was liquidated or dissolved.

7010	Month	Day	Year
	1		

(c) 0180 **1** ☐ This U.S. business enterprise is a U.S. affiliate of a foreign person or entity, but became a U.S. affiliate after the end of its fiscal year that ended in calendar year 2009, or if a newly formed company, its first fiscal year did not or will not end until after the end of calendar year 2009. *Complete items (1) and (2) below.*

(1) *Give date when the U.S. business enterprise became a U.S. affiliate of a foreign person.*

7013	Month	Day	Year
	1		

(2) *Give the ending date of the U.S. business enterprise's fiscal year that ended in calendar year 2009. If a newly formed company give the ending date of the U.S. business enterprise's first fiscal year. NOTE: For a newly formed company this must be a date in calendar year 2010.*

7014	Month	Day	Year
	1		

(d) This U.S. business enterprise was a U.S. affiliate of a foreign person or entity during the fiscal year that ended in calendar year 2009 but was (please check appropriate box (1) or (2)):

(1) 0112 **1** ☐ **Fully consolidated** into the 2009 BE-15 report filed for another U.S. affiliate; **OR** **(2)** 0112 **2** ☐ **Merged** into another U.S. affiliate and its operations are included on the 2009 BE-15 report filed for the other U.S. affiliate.

On the lines below give the name, address, and BEA Identification Number of the U.S. affiliate into which this U.S. affiliate is fully consolidated or merged.

Name
0120 | 0

Street or P.O. Box
0130 | 0

City	State	ZIP Code
0140	0	0141	0	0150	0

BEA Identification Number of the U.S. affiliate into which this U.S. affiliate is fully consolidated or merged.
7011 | 0

(e) 0190 **1** ☐ Other – *Specify and include reference to section of regulations or instructions on which claim is based.*

7015 | 0

Remarks

Authority – This survey is being conducted under the International Investment and Trade in Services Survey Act (P.L. 94-472, 90 Stat. 2059, 22 U.S.C. 3101-3108, as amended), and the filing of reports is MANDATORY pursuant to Section 5(b)(2) of the Act (22 U.S.C. 3104). The implementing regulations are contained in Title 15, CFR, Part 806.

Penalties – Whoever fails to report may be subject to a civil penalty of not less than $2,500, and not more than $25,000, and to injunctive relief commanding such person to comply, or both. The civil penalties are subject to inflationary adjustments. Those adjustments are found in 15 CFR 6.4. Whoever willfully fails to report shall be fined not more than $10,000 and, if an individual, may be imprisoned for not more than one year, or both. Any officer, director, employee, or agent of any corporation who knowingly participates in such violation, upon conviction, may be punished by a like fine, imprisonment, or both. (22 U.S.C. 3105)

Notwithstanding any other provision of the law, no person is required to respond to, nor shall any person be subject to a penalty for failure to comply with, a collection of information subject to the requirements of the Paperwork Reduction Act, unless that collection of information displays a currently valid OMB Control Number. The control number for this survey is at the top of page 1 of this form.

Respondent Burden – Public reporting burden for this form is estimated to vary from 20 to 75 minutes per response with an average of 1 hour per response, including the time for reviewing instructions, searching existing data sources, gathering and maintaining the data needed, and completing and reviewing the collection of information. Send comments regarding this burden estimate or any other aspect of this collection of information, including suggestions for reducing this burden, to: Director, Bureau of Economic Analysis (BE-1), U.S. Department of Commerce, Washington, DC 20230; and to the Office of Management and Budget, Paperwork Reduction Project 0608-0034, Washington, DC 20503.

Confidentiality – The Act provides that your report to this Bureau is CONFIDENTIAL and may be used only for analytical or statistical purposes. Without your prior written permission, the information filed in your report CANNOT be presented in a manner that allows it to be individually identified. Your report CANNOT be used for purposes of taxation, investigation, or regulation. Copies retained in your files are immune from legal process.

DEFINITIONS OF KEY TERMS

Affiliate means a business enterprise located in one country that is directly or indirectly owned or controlled by a person or entity of another country to the extent of 10 percent or more of its voting stock for an incorporated business or an equivalent interest for an unincorporated business, including a branch.

Direct investment means the ownership or control, directly or indirectly, by one person or entity of 10 percent or more of the voting securities of an incorporated business enterprise or an equivalent interest in an unincorporated business enterprise.

U.S. affiliate means an affiliate located in the United States in which a foreign person or entity has a direct investment.

Table 3
WHICH BE-15 FORM TO FILE

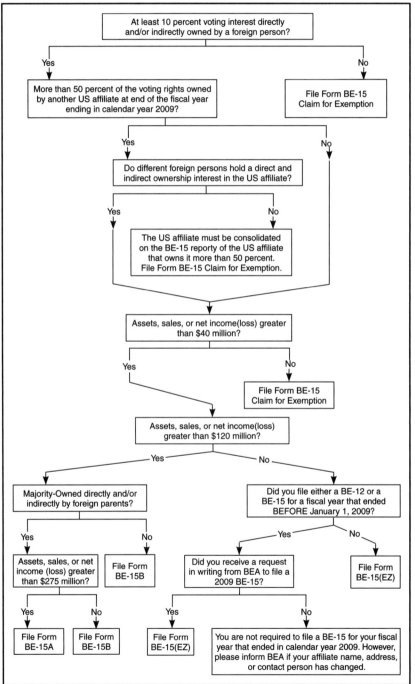

At least 10 percent voting interest directly and/or indirectly owned by a foreign person?

Yes → More than 50 percent of the voting rights owned by another US affiliate at end of the fiscal year ending in calendar year 2009?

No → File Form BE-15 Claim for Exemption

Yes → Do different foreign persons hold a direct and indirect ownership interest in the US affiliate?

No → The US affiliate must be consolidated on the BE-15 reporty of the US affiliate that owns it more than 50 percent. File Form BE-15 Claim for Exemption.

Assets, sales, or net income(loss) greater than $40 million?

Yes / No → File Form BE-15 Claim for Exemption

Assets, sales, or net income(loss) greater than $120 million?

Yes → Majority-Owned directly and/or indirectly by foreign parents?

No → Did you file either a BE-12 or a BE-15 for a fiscal year that ended BEFORE January 1, 2009?

Yes → Assets, sales, or net income (loss) greater than $275 million?

No → File Form BE-15B

Yes → Did you receive a request in writing from BEA to file a 2009 BE-15?

No → File Form BE-15(EZ)

Yes → File Form BE-15A

No → File Form BE-15B

Yes → File Form BE-15(EZ)

No → You are not required to file a BE-15 for your fiscal year that ended in calendar year 2009. However, please inform BEA if your affiliate name, address, or contact person has changed.

Source: "Which BE-15 Form to File?" U.S. Bureau of Economic Analysis, accessed March 4, 2011, www.bea.gov/surveys/pdf/form-trans-2009.pdf

2.1 Title insurance

While buying real estate in the US is a somewhat different process, it is basically similar to Canada and easy to do. The ease with which property can be bought in the US can be both a good and bad thing. The ease in which real estate can be purchased leads investors to think that there are no problems. The problem is that there are no warning signals when you do something the wrong way; it is just as easy to buy the property the wrong way as it is to buy it the right way. In other words, there is nothing prohibiting you from doing things the wrong way. See Chapter 2 for a discussion of the various ways to purchase property in the US, as well as the pros and cons of each.

Other than how you own the property, the biggest difference between buying real estate in the US and Canada is title insurance. Wikipedia defines title insurance as "indemnity insurance against financial loss from defects in title to real property and from the invalidity or unenforceability of mortgage liens." The insurance policy will protect an owner's interest in the real estate against loss due to title defects or liens. The insurance will defend against a lawsuit attacking the title, or reimburse the insured for the actual monetary loss incurred, up to the dollar amount of insurance provided by the policy, which is typically the purchase price of the property.

Although the cost of title insurance varies from state to state and the calculations involve numerous variables, the rule of thumb cost is approximately 0.5 percent of the purchase price of the property, which is a one-time cost. The cost of insurance is typically paid by the seller, but is subject to negotiation.

First American and Fidelity National Title Insurance Company are the two largest title companies; combined they account for more than 55 percent of the market.

2.2 Finding a real estate agent

One of the biggest mistakes real estate investors make is to buy without the use of a buyer's agent who is experienced in working with real estate investors. Buyers' agents are different from other real estate agents or brokers in that they do not represent sellers; some never list properties for sale and only work with buyers.

When a buyer calls the listing agent asking to see the property and eventually has that agent draw up an offer on that property, the buyer is in effect asking that agent to represent both the buyer and seller at the same time. This obviously sets up a conflict of interest called "dual agency." Some states ban dual agency, and all states require disclosures of the conflict.

To be clear, an agent has a fiduciary duty to act in the client's best interest at all times. Many would say it is impossible to work in the seller's best interest of wanting to get the best (highest) price, while at the same time, work in the buyer's best interest of wanting to get the best (lowest) price.

You can find a buyer's agent at the National Buyer's Agent Association at http://buyersagent.net.

Note: The closing costs in the US are quite a bit higher than those in Canada due to a number of fees, taxes, and insurance costs that are typically rolled into the closing costs. Possible costs include pro-rata property taxes, insurance, appraisal, and inspection fees. However, attorneys are not needed and generally not used in the US.

2.3 US mortgages

There are US lenders that will provide mortgages to Canadians buying property in the US. Granted, there is not a large number of mortgage providers for Canadians, but there are enough to give you the ability to shop for rates and terms.

As I mentioned in Chapter 4, liabilities (mortgages) do not typically reduce your US taxable estate unless the mortgage is a non-recourse mortgage. RBC offers a non-recourse mortgage for those that it would benefit. For some investors, this may be the simplest way to avoid US nonresident estate tax.

RBC tells me that the non-recourse mortgage has an interest rate that is 0.5 to 1 percent higher than its traditional mortgage rate. The reason for the higher interest rate is that the bank is assuming more risk with a non-recourse mortgage; the bank does not have recourse to come after your other assets if you do not pay, since the bank's recourse is limited to the property.

Some of the things you should know about obtaining a US mortgage is that different rules apply to a person looking to buy a second (vacation) home versus a person looking at a property for investment. The rates and terms will be better for a second home than for an investment property. In addition, some lenders will not lend on investment property, but those that do will require a minimum down payment of 30 to 50 percent. Some lenders may require a liquid reserve of 3 to 12 months, determined on a case-by-case basis.

Some lenders you might consider talking to include:

➤ RBC: 1-800-236-8872

➤ Natbank (Parent company is National Bank of Canada): 954-781-4005

➤ Desjardins: 1-800-454-5058

➤ Harris Trust (Parent company is Bank of Montreal): 480-951-9670 (AZ), 1-800-421-2435 (FL)

➤ HSBC: 1-800-333-7023

2.4 Foreign currency

Talking about mortgages naturally leads into foreign currency discussions because you may run into an issue of having a mortgage (debt) in Canadian dollars, but having mortgage payments (revenue and assets) in US dollars. When you have a situation of having to pay the Canadian mortgage every month with US dollars, you are at the whim of the currency markets. As I see it, there are three ways to reduce or eliminate that risk:

➤ Pay with cash.

➤ Use other Canadian money to pay the Canadian mortgage.

➤ Use a US mortgage.

Of course, if the rent does not cover all of the rental expenses (have positive cash flow), you have the same problem in reverse because you are continually sending money to the states to cover expenses.

A related issue is the expense of converting currency, which is especially acute when continually transferring small amounts of money. There are really two ways in which to transfer money across the border — to send checks or wire transfers. Sending checks can be problematic in that there may be additional bank fees for accepting checks drawn on a foreign bank and there may be holds placed on the checks. In my opinion, wire transfers are the best way to go; there are little to no hassles and it is faster. When making wire transfers, there are basically two ways to go about it; you let your bank or brokerage be your currency broker or you can use a firm that specializes in currency exchange. It has been my experience that currency brokers are the best choice because they are typically less expensive and easier to deal with. I recommend Moneycorp, a large currency exchange firm out of the UK. Moneycorp is the firm to which RBC refers clients. You can find a link to Moneycorp on my firm's site at www.keatsconnelly.com. We have negotiated substantial discounts for anyone using the portal on our site.

Another choice is Custom House Currency (part of Western Union) for your currency exchange needs. They can be found at www.customhouse.com. Custom House Currency has a currency exchange service called Online FX that is easy to use, or you can call 1-866-430-5386.

3. Hiring a Property Manager

As an owner of one or more rental homes located thousands of miles away, you should definitely consider hiring a local property manager. The place to start looking for competent property managers is at the Institute of Real Estate Management (IREM). IREM issues the Certified Property Management (CPM) designation (www.irem.org). You can interview potential managers by asking for referrals from your real estate agent.

Sample 14 includes some questions you should ask potential property managers.

In addition, your realtor can provide recommendations for a property manager but you can also search for managers at www.allpropertymanagement.com. All Property Management allows you to search by type of property and zip code.

Sample 14
QUESTIONS TO ASK POTENTIAL PROPERTY MANAGERS

1. Are you paying the real estate agent a fee or commission if I use your services? (In other words, how objective was your agent in making this referral?)

2. How long have you been a property manager and can your provide me with referrals?

3. How many properties do you manage?

4. How many Canadian owners do you manage properties for?

5. What staff do you have? Do you do all of this yourself, or do you have employees, or do you outsource some of the work?

6. Can I have sample agreements to review? You will want to review the rental agreement and the agreement between you and the property manager.

7. How are your fees calculated? Are the fees guaranteed for a period of time?

8. Am I locked into this agreement for some period of time, or can I leave at any time?

9. Will you provide me with copies of all receipts and a full accounting monthly?

10. What fees if any do you charge while the property is empty?

11. Will I have final say on all tenants?

12. What are the rules involving the eviction of a tenant?

13. What is the process of evicting a tenant, if necessary? Do you have a relationship with an attorney that can assist with questions in this area? Who pays for the attorney when you ask questions?

Conclusion

My sincere hope is that I have made the topic of buying real estate in the US (and the tax effects thereof) a little less confusing. For a Canadian, buying real estate in the US is relatively easy, so much so that many investors have a false sense of security. There are many things to consider and numerous ways in which things can go wrong.

My goal has been to educate you on the major issues that confront nearly every Canadian investor in US real estate. I briefly explained the opportunity, the buying process, talked about US mortgages, direct and indirect ownership methods, income tax, estate tax, and other things you should know. This book attempted to answer the major questions Canadian investors and their advisers have about buying real estate in the US; those questions included:

➤ How should I own the property?

➤ What are the tax consequences and how do I minimize my tax liability?

➤ How do I report the income on my tax returns?

➤ How do I avoid US estate tax?

➤ What are my tax filing requirements?

I have tried to incorporate both technical and practical issues and explanations, by giving helpful hints, cautions, and examples.

Although I have done my best to take a complex set of laws and explain them in some detail, I do not suggest that you attempt to do it yourself. There is an important distinction between knowledge and wisdom. Wisdom is defined as the ability to make sensible decisions and judgments based on personal knowledge and experience. I have attempted to impart knowledge, but knowledge without experience frequently turns into folly.

When I was younger and had more time, I loved to play chess. I read many books written by chess grandmasters on the subject. Even though I have read the books (knowledge) and played the games (experience), I have never been able to call myself an expert at chess. Just like my chess analogy, you cannot expect to read a book and perform at the level necessary for success. You need an experienced professional to make sense of and to provide advice on the nuances of each situation.

Please seek out knowledgeable and experienced professionals when needed — your return on investment may well exceed that of the real estate you are buying.

I wish you success in all of your investments!

★ ★

Appendix I: Checklist for Buying Real Estate in the US

Educate yourself about what is involved with owning real estate in another country, such as the following:

❑ Income taxes (how much, when, and how paid)?

❑ Nonresident estate taxes (Will they apply to you? If so, find out how to avoid.)

❑ Decide how best to own the property (see Chapter 2).

❑ Learn what sort of non-tax reporting is required by Canada and the US.

❑ Locate an experienced cross-border tax professional.

❑ If necessary, have an attorney establish the proper US business entity to hold the property.

❑ Obtain Employer Identification Number (EIN) and/or Individual Taxpayer Identification Number (ITIN), as appropriate.

❑ Locate an experienced realtor that also has experience working with Canadians.

- [ ] If needed, identify lending sources.

- [ ] If renting, locate a property manager experienced with foreign buyers.

- [ ] Purchase real estate.

- [ ] If property is being rented, submit Certificate of Foreign Person's Claim That Income Is Effectively Connected with the Conduct of a Trade or Business in the United States (Form W-8ECI) to the property manager or tenant.

- [ ] Complete withholding forms: Annual Return for Partnership Withholding Tax (Form 8804), Foreign Partner's Information Statement of Section 1446 Withholding Tax (Form 8805), and Partnership Withholding Tax Payment Voucher (Form 8813), as necessary.

- [ ] If a US entity was used to purchase the property, the entity must file a tax return by March 15 for corporations and April 15 for partnerships. A revocable living trust is not required to file a tax return; all income is reported on your individual tax return.

- [ ] If the property was rented, in nearly all cases, you will need to file US Nonresident Alien Income Tax Return (Form 1040NR) by June 15 of each year.

- [ ] File Bureau of Economic Analysis Survey of Foreign Direct Investment in the US (Form BE-15) by May 31 or by February 15 for Transactions of US Affiliate, Except a US Banking Affiliate, with Foreign Parent (BE-605), if required.

- [ ] When selling a property that exceeds $300,000, look into the necessity of filing Application for Withholding Certificate for Dispositions by Foreign Persons of the US Real Property Interests (Form 8288-B) to reduce the withholding tax.

Appendix II: Resources

Cross Border Tax Help

- Keats, Connelly and Associates, LLC: www.keatsconnelly.com

- Cross Border Tax & Accounting, LLC: www.cbta.net

US Tax Resources

- Internal Revenue Service (IRS): www.irs.gov

- IRS Publications:

  - Publication 515: Withholding of Tax on Non-resident Aliens and Foreign Entities: www.irs.gov/pub/irs-pdf/p515.pdf

  - Publication 597: US—Canada Income Tax Treaty: www.irs.gov/pub/irs-pdf/p597.pdf

  - Foreign Investment in Real Property Tax Act: www.irs.gov/privacy/article/0,,id=160733,00.html

✦ US Department of Commerce Bureau of Economic Analysis (BEA): www.bea.gov

Realtor Associations:

✦ National Association of Realtors: www.realtor.org

✦ Arizona Association of Realtors: http://aaronline.com

✦ California Association of Realtors: www.car.org

✦ Florida Realtors: www.floridarealtors.org

✦ Nevada Association of Realtors: www.nvar.org

Realtors known to work with Canadians:

✦ *Phoenix:*

  ✦ Richard Bazinet — Wild West Real Estate: www.wildwestrealestate.us

  ✦ David Boyd — Aliya Investments: www.aliyainvestments.com

  ✦ Linda Gerchick — US Investment Realty: www.justsoldit.com

  ✦ Krista Kennedy — John Hall: http://kristakennedy.com

  ✦ Diane Olson — Home Smart: www.dianeolson.ca

  ✦ Maureen Porter — Arizona for Canadians: www.arizonaforcanadians.com

  ✦ Mike Smith — Phoenix Native Properties: www.phoenixnative.com

✦ *Palm Springs:*

  ✦ Paul Kaplan — Modern Real Estate Group: www.paulkaplanrealtor.com/ForeignBuyers.php

- Claudine Messik — Keller Williams: www.claudinereal.com/Real_Estate_in_Palm_Springs_for_Canadians.htm

- Dick Sakowicz — Re/Max: www.dicksakowicz.com/buyer-guide-for-canadians.php

- *South Florida*

  - Shant Epremian — Keller Williams: www.bocaratonluxuryhomes.net

Canadian Tax Resources

- Canada Revenue Agency (CRA): www.cra-arc.gc.ca

- Report of foreign holdings — Foreign Income Verification Statement (Form T1135): www.cra-arc.gc.ca/E/pbg/tf/t1135/README.html

About the Author

Since he was young, Dale Walters has had a passion for helping others. He considered both the traditionally helpful fields of law and medicine, but his natural talent for numbers led him into accounting, an industry that helps people with some of the hardest decisions in their lives — financial decisions.

He has been helping people with their financial decisions since 1980. Along the way, Walters earned both the US Certified Financial Planner™ (CFP®) and Certified Public Accountant designations, and even spent time in the tax department of the "Big Four" accounting firm of KPMG.

Walters' life has been a series of fortunate events. Working at KPMG was no different. While there, he got involved with preparing international tax returns of foreign individuals working in the Phoenix offices of Motorola. After a few years with KPMG, Walters went to work for a small CPA firm in Scottsdale, Arizona. This led him to a fateful meeting with Bob Keats and Tom Connelly, founders of Keats, Connelly and Associates, a leading wealth-management firm focused on helping people live on both sides of the border. Within six months he joined their team.

In keeping with the fortunate events in his life, working at Keats, Connelly and Associates afforded Walters a mentor in Bob Keats. In addition to being a dual citizen of the United States and Canada, and one of the top cross-border advisors, Keats is also the author of *The Border Guide*, a Canadian best-selling book focused on living, working, investing, and retiring on both sides of the border. Armed with his mentor, Walters earned his Canadian CFP® designation, making him one of the very first people to hold designations on both sides of the border, and by 2004, he was named the CEO of the firm.

Since joining the leadership team of Keats, Connelly and Associates with Keats, Walters has helped the firm earn Ethics Awards, community volunteerism awards, workplace flexibility awards, and even impact awards for being one of the top businesses in Arizona. The firm has also been named a top firm in the nation by *CPA Wealth Provider* magazine on more than one occasion, and has opened additional offices throughout North America.

On the personal side, Walters has a passion for both wrestling and martial arts. Both passions have served him well. Wrestling helped him to earn him a college scholarship back in the 1970s, which led to meeting his wife of three decades, which led him to being a dad of two wonderful children. Martial arts helped him achieve inner peace as well as World Heavyweight Karate championships from 1986 to 1989.

Both personally and as part of a company, his greatest rewards continue to come from helping people. That is ultimately why he wrote this book; to help you avoid the many potential mistakes that can be made when buying real estate in the United States.